Maths *Key Stage 1*
Teacher's Resource Book

Published in 2002 by:
Nelson Thornes Ltd
Delta Place
27 Bath Road
CHELTENHAM
GL53 7TH
United Kingdom

01 02 03 04 05 / 10 9 8 7 6 5 4 3 2 1

A catalogue record for this book is available from the British Library

ISBN 0 7487 6370 8

Printed and bound in Great Britain by The Bath Press

This publication contains material from the National Numeracy Strategy
Framework for Teaching Mathematics, produced by the Department for Education
and Employment, 1999. (Crown copyright. Reproduced under the terms of HMSO
Guidance Note 8.)

Nelson Thornes publishes a comprehensive range of teacher resource books in the *Blueprints* and *Learning Targets* series. These titles provide busy teachers with unbeatable curriculum coverage, inspiration and value for money. For a complete list, please call our Primary Customer Services on 01242 267280, send an e-mail to cservices@nelsonthornes.com or write to:

Nelson Thornes Ltd, Freepost, Primary Customer Services, Delta Place, 27 Bath Road, Cheltenham GL53 7ZZ.

All Nelson Thornes titles can be bought by phone using a credit or debit card on 01242 267280 or online by visiting our website – www.nelsonthornes.com

Contents

Contents

Introduction

Mathematics has seen many changes since the introduction of the National Curriculum and the National Numeracy Strategy (NNS). The sequence of teaching number work has been tuned in some detail and is now clearly defined. Mental arithmetic has been given some prominence, particularly with early work on establishing understanding of numbers. Most significantly, the maths curriculum has a clarity through the NNS, which should help all teachers promote maths very strongly. Of course, most schools had a similar curriculum in place previously and all good teachers very often taught lessons in a similar style to that which has been promoted in recent years. Nevertheless, the clear curriculum objectives and the examples offered in the NNS documentation are very useful to teachers and planners.

It needs to be said that the NNS is applicable to different schools in different ways. In some schools, the way the NNS is set out is not helpful. Others schools can work ahead of the suggested timetables and many will want to give an emphasis in their own ways that suit their school. This is acknowledged within the NNS and the same applies to the contents of this book. Activities designated as Year 1 may sometimes be carried out in Foundation or sometimes in Year 2; it all depends on the children's abilities and what they are ready for. Likewise for the Year 2 work. Please adapt as necessary.

The activities contained within this book often contain differentiation but teachers may want to modify them to suit their own purpose. This is right and proper; classes that had three ability groups often have five now, with at least as much emphasis being given to the more able children as used to be given to the less able ones. Please differentiate as much as you like.

Finally, the opportunities for good teaching of mathematics to a high standard and in an enjoyable way are endless. The activities in this book are designed to be used in an exciting way, which will provide the most important factor – motivation to learn more.

Activity sheets

Each activity page in *Blueprints Maths Key Stage 1: Teacher's Resource Book* is linked to an activity sheet in *Blueprints Maths Key Stage 1: Pupil Resource Book*. The link is made explicit through the numbers in the hand prints in each book. Each activity sheet is designed to assist the theme and is offered as a possible activity in order to save preparation time. You, the teacher, may wish to use others or devise your own.

It should also be noted that not all the activity sheets include explicit instructions for the children to follow. Such instructions that do appear can only be abbreviated guidelines. Irrespective of any printed instruction, the children will, of course, follow your own instructions and explanations of the activity they are to undertake.

A small number of activity sheets are not directly related to the National Numeracy Strategy but relate to the inclusion of the number 31 as a developmental point between knowledge of numbers to 20 (Year 1) and 100 (Year 2). This has been done because many teachers find the jump from 20 to 100 to be rather large for some children and a stepping stone is helpful. Thirty-one is sometimes used as this stepping stone because it is often the number in an infant class (including the teacher) and can therefore be used for various counting, addition and subtraction games. It is also the maximum number of days in a month and the children will know the numbers because of important events, especially birthdays and, finally, it crosses the boundary between the twenties numbers which are usually well known and the thirties, the next major step in developing towards 100.

Resources

The National Numeracy Strategy encourages teachers to use a wide range of resources. It is appreciated that some infant classrooms are extremely well equipped and may have all the resources needed for the entire Key Stage. The activities in *Blueprints Maths Key Stage 1: Teacher's Resource Book* sometimes indicate resources that might be considered to be extra to those used in everyday teaching and may, therefore, have to be sought out from colleagues or the resource centre. It is usually only these 'extras' that are listed under the heading Resources; it will be appreciated that this list is only a guide and cannot be exhaustive.

Introduction

Activity sheet number in the hand print in the *Pupil Resource Book*
also on the relevant page (top left) in the *Teacher's Resource Book*

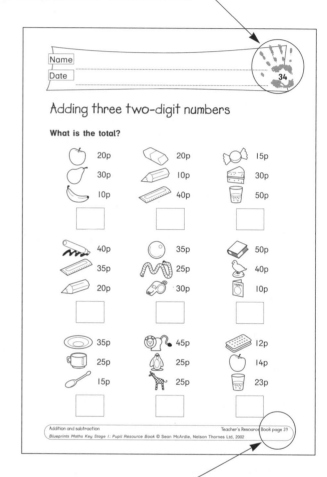

Linked *Teacher's Resource Book* page number appears
in the bottom-right corner of the relevant activity sheet
in the *Pupil Resource Book*

NNS curriculum planner

Reference Statement in NNS Section 3 Yearly teaching programmes and planning grids (Blueprints activity page/activity sheet headings)	NNS suggested Year	Reference page in NNS Section 3 Yearly teaching programmes and planning grids	Reference page in NNS Section 5 Supplement of Examples	Reference page in Blueprints Maths KS1: Teacher's Resource Book	Activity sheet in Blueprints Maths KS1: Pupil Resource Book
Number names to 20	1	6	8	2	1
Number names to 31	1 (Not part of NNS programme)			3	2
Number names to 100	2	10	9	4	3
Counting to 20/31	1 (Not part of NNS programme)			5	4
Counting to 100	2	10	3	6	5
Counting in ones/tens and hundreds	2	10	3	7	6
Counting from any two-digit number	2	10	3, 5, 7	8	7
Counting in twos	2	10	3, 5, 7	9	8
Odds and evens	2	10	3, 5, 7	10	9
Steps of five and three	2	10	3, 5, 7	11	10
Steps of three, four and five	3	14	3, 5, 7	12	11
Multiples of 2, 5 and 10	3	14	7	13	12
Read and write numbers 20/100	2	10	9	15	13
Partitioning	1	6	8	16	14
	2	10	9	16	14
	3	14	9	16	14
0 as place holder	2	10	9	17	15
Reinforcing activities	1 and 2	6 and 10	8–15	18	16
Comparing and ordering	1	6	10	20	17
	2	10	11	20	17
Ordinal numbers	R	2	13	21	18
	2	10	11	21	18
More than, less than, between	1	6	10	22	19
	2	10	11	22	19
The = sign and comparing	1	6	10	23	20
	2	10	11	23	20
One more or less	1	6	12	24	21
	2	10	13	24	21
Ten or hundred more or less	1	6	12	25	22
	2	10	12	25	22
	3	14	13	25	22
Order whole numbers to 100	1	6	14	26	23
	2	10	15	26	23
Sensible guesses to 20/50, vocabulary	1	6	16	28	24
	2	10	17	28	24
Rounding to nearest ten	2	10	19	29	25
Half and quarter	2	10	21, 23	31	26
Equivalence	2	10	23	32	27
Understanding addition	1	6	24, 26	34	28
	2	10	25, 27	34	28
Addition in any order	1	6	24, 28	35	29
	2	10	25, 27	35	29
Using the + sign	1	6	24, 26	35	30
	2	10	25, 27	35	30
Number sentences	1	6	24, 26, 28	36	31
	2	10	25, 27, 29	36	31

NNS curriculum planner

Reference Statement in NNS Section 3 Yearly teaching programmes and planning grids (Blueprints activity page/activity sheet headings)	NNS suggested Year	Reference page in NNS Section 3 Yearly teaching programmes and planning grids	Reference page in NNS Section 5 Supplement of Examples	Reference page in Blueprints Maths KS1: Teacher's Resource Book	Activity sheet in Blueprints Maths KS1: Pupil Resource Book
Symbols for unknown numbers	1	6	24, 26, 28	37	32
	2	10	25, 27, 29	37	32
Adding two or more numbers	1	6	26	38	33
	2	10	27	38	33
Adding three two-digit numbers	2	10	27	39	34
Understanding subtraction	1	6	24, 28	40	35
	2	10	25, 29	40	35
Vocabulary of subtraction	2	10	25, 29	41	36
The − sign; symbols for unknown numbers	1	6	24, 28	42	37
	2	10	25, 29	42	37
Recording calculations using symbols	1	6	24, 28	43	38
	2	10	25, 29	43	38
Using symbols in number sentences	1	6	24, 28	44	39
	2	10	25, 29	44	39
Addition/subtraction as inverse operations	2	10	25, 29	45	40
Addition in different order	2	10	59	47	41
Checking	2	10	59	47	42
Number pairs totalling ten/bond bingo	1	6	30	49	43
Multiples of 10 totalling 100	2	10	31	50	44
Addition doubles and halves to 10	1	6	30	51	45
Subtraction facts to 10	1	6	30	52	46
Number bonds to 10 (+ and −)	1	6	30	53	47
2× and 10× tables	2	10	53	54	48
Multiplication facts for 5× table	2	10	53	55	49
Division, 2×, 10× tables	2	10	53	56	50
10-multiples halves	2	10	53	56	50
Doubles to 15	2	10	53	57	51
Doubles of multiples of 5	2	10	53	57	51
Multiplication as repeated addition	2	10	47, 49	59	52
Division as grouping	2	10	47, 49	60	53
Multiply and divide with confidence	2	10	47, 49	61	54
Choosing operations	1	7	60	62	55
	2	11	61	62	55
Efficient methods	2	10	61	62	55
Solve simple puzzles and problems	1	7	62	64	56
	2	11	63	64	56
Explain how problems are solved	1	7	64	66	57
	2	11	65	66	57
Patterns and relationships	1	7	62	67	58
	2	11	63	67	58
Explain in writing and orally	1	7	64 (orally)	68	59
	2	11	65	68	59
Solving 'real life' problems	1	7	66, 68, 70	70	60
	2	11	67, 69, 71	70	60
Recognise coins of different values	1	7	68	72	61
	2	11	69	72	61

NNS curriculum planner

Reference Statement in NNS Section 3 Yearly teaching programmes and planning grids (Blueprints activity page/activity sheet headings)	NNS suggested Year	Reference page in NNS Section 3 Yearly teaching programmes and planning grids	Reference page in NNS Section 5 Supplement of Examples	Reference page in Blueprints Maths KS1: Teacher's Resource Book	Activity sheet in Blueprints Maths KS1: Pupil Resource Book
Find total, give change	1	7	68	73	62
	2	11	69	73	62
Choose which coins	1	7	68	73	63
	2	11	69	73	63
Paying exact sums using small coins	1	7	68	74	64
	2	11	69	74	64
Translate between pounds and pennies	2	11	69	75	65
Sort objects – lists and tables	1	7	90, 92	77	66
	2	11	91, 93	77	66
Sort and classify – pictures/pictograms	1	7	90, 92	78	67
	2	11	91, 93	78	67
Sort and classify – lists	1	7	90, 92	79	68
	2	11	91, 93	79	68
Simple block graphs	2	11	91, 93	80	69
Estimate, measure, compare size	1	7	74, 76	82	70
	2	11	73, 75	82	70
Estimate, measure, compare size/capacity	1	7	74, 76	83	71
	2	11	73, 75	83	71
Read simple scales to nearest division	2	11	77	84	72
Measure/draw to the nearest centimetre	2	11	77	85	73
Vocabulary of time	1	7	78	86	74
	2	11	79	86	74
Use units of time	1	7	78	87	75
	2	11	79	87	75
Order events in time	1	7	78	88	76
	2	11	79	88	76
Days of week, seasons, months	1	7	78	89	77
	2	11	79	89	77
Read time to hour/half-hour (analogue)	1	7	78	90	78
Read quarter-hours (analogue)	2	11	79	91	79
Mathematical names for 2-D/3-D shapes	2	11	81	93	80
Make models, patterns and pictures	1	7	82	94	81
Sort shapes and describe features	2	11	81	95	82
Folding shapes and beginning symmetry	1	7	82	96	83
Line symmetry	2	11	85	97	84
Describe position, direction, movement	1	7	86, 88	98	85
	2	11	87, 89	98	85
Turning clockwise/anticlockwise	1	7	88	99	86
	2	11	87, 89	99	86
Right angles	2	11	89	100	87

Note: R represents Reception. The NNS uses this designation. It is understood that the term 'Foundation Stage' is now being used as an alternative.

Occasional references relate to Year 3 although this is not part of the NNS Key Stage 1 work. This is because many schools will advance work when appropriate with able and more able children and will include elements of Year 3 work.

Scottish 5–14 curriculum planner

NUMBER, MONEY AND MEASUREMENT		
LEVEL A	**LEVEL B**	**LEVEL C**
Range and type of numbers	**Range and type of numbers**	**Add and subtract**
Whole number 0–20 *Pages* 2, 23, 24 (37, 42), 43 Halves *Page* 31	Whole numbers to 100 then 1000 *Pages* 3–7, 10, 15–18, 20–26, 40, 41 Quarters *Pages* 31, 32	Mentally for one digit to or from three digits *Pages* 38, 39 Mentally for subtraction by 'adding on' *Pages* 38, 39
Money	**Money**	
Using 1p–20p *Page* 74	Coins up to £1 *Pages* 72, 73	
Add and subtract	**Add and subtract**	
Mentally 0–10 *Pages* 40, 41, 49, 52, 53	0–20 *Pages* 20, 21, 22, 23, 24, 40, 41, 45, 47, 49 Without calculator (two digits) *Pages* 8, 9, 11, 12, 25, 35, 36, 70 Application in number, measurement, money, change to £1 *Pages* 72, 73, 74	
Patterns and sequences		
Copy and describe simple patterns or sequences of objects *Page* 94		
Measure and estimate	**Multiply and divide**	
Length, weight, area, volume *Pages* 85, 86 Place pairs of objects in order *Pages* 83, 84 Estimate length in convenient non-standard units *Pages* 83, 84 Use and understand vocabulary related to all aspects of measuring *Pages* 83, 84, 85	Mentally by 2, 3, 4, 5, 10 *Pages* 13, 50, 51, 54, 55, 56, 57, 59, 60, 61, 62 Without calculator for two-digit numbers 2, 3, 4, 5, 10 *Pages* 57, 59, 62, 64	
	Round numbers	
	To nearest ten *Page* 29	
Time	**Fractions, percentages, ratio**	
Place events in time sequences *Pages* 86, 87, 88, 89 Time activities in non-standard units *Page* 86 Tell time in hours – analogue and digital *Page* 90	Halves and quarters, one- and two-digit numbers *Page* 32	
	Patterns and sequences	
	Whole numbers within 100 *Page* 66 More complex sequences with shape *Pages* 67, 68	
	Functions and equations	
	Find missing numbers where symbols are used *Pages* 37, 42, 44, 61, 64	
	Measure and estimate	
	Length: m, $\frac{1}{2}$ m, $\frac{1}{4}$ m, cm *Pages* 85, 86 Read scales to nearest graduation *Page* 84	
	Time	
	Place events in time sequence *Pages* 86, 87, 88, 89 Tell time using analogue, quarter, half past *Pages* 90, 91 Read time in hours and minutes using digital display *Page* 91	

Scottish 5–14 curriculum planner

INFORMATION HANDLING		
LEVEL A	**LEVEL B**	**LEVEL C**
Collect	**Organise**	
By obtaining information *Page 77* By collecting information *Pages 77, 78, 79*	By using a tally sheet *Page 79*	
Organise	**Display**	
By sorting into specific sets *Pages 78, 79*	By using tables, charts or diagrams *Page 79* By constructing a bar graph *Page 80*	
Display	**Interpret**	
By drawing simple diagrams *Pages 78, 79*	From displays *Page 79*	
Interpret		
From display *Page 79*		

Scottish 5–14 curriculum planner

SHAPE, POSITION AND MOVEMENT		
LEVEL A	**LEVEL B**	**LEVEL C**
Range of shapes	**Range of shapes**	
Collect, discuss, make and use 2-D and 3-D shapes *Page 93* Classify shapes by simple properties *Pages 93, 95* Identify and name cubes, cuboids, cylinders, spheres *Pages 93, 95* Identify and name squares, rectangles, triangles and circles *Pages 93, 94, 95* Create or copy 3-D structures *Page 93*	Respond to descriptions of shapes referring to faces, edges, corners, sides, angles *Page 95*	
	Position and movement	
	Give and understand instruction to turn through right angles *Pages 99, 100*	
	Symmetry	
Position and movement	Recognise symmetrical shapes by folding or mirrors *Pages 96, 97*	
Associated with position of object *Pages 98, 99*	**Angles**	
	Use template to draw or check for a right angle *Page 100*	

Links with other subjects

Literacy

Mathematics has always been acknowledged as a language in its own right but it should also be seen as a way of linking with the English work that is also taking place in school. In many areas of maths – shape, measure, position, angle – opportunities exist to make word banks that can be exhibited in a special maths area or may be included as part of a general class bank. Children often keep their own word banks in personal 'dictionaries'. These ideas should be encouraged and link strongly with most other subjects where similar banks may be constructed.

Spelling of mathematical words can be difficult because they tend not to be seen with the same frequency as other language. However, the same rules of spelling apply and children must be encouraged to spell mathematical vocabulary correctly. A note of warning – it needs to be clearly understood that although spelling is important, it should not detract from the mathematical objective of a lesson. Why not include mathematical words in the weekly spellings homework?

Science

Science connects with mathematics in very practical ways. Indeed, much science work would be virtually impossible unless children could apply the four rules properly, understand and use symbolism, recognise and work with negative numbers and be aware of different forms of representing and interrogating data. It sometimes looks as if the link is just with drawing graphs but this is to underestimate the importance of data.

As with maths, scientific data is only useful when analysed for meaning (Investigating Skills). Children need to measure accurately in science with rulers and other instruments. They also need to be aware of a range of standard units – cm, km, g, kg, ml and l, at least. Negative numbers will play small part in science at Key Stage 1 but may occur if temperatures are being discussed as part of a project on growing plants for example. Work on forces and motion will include opportunities for discussing position and direction.

ICT

The widespread availability of PCs in most primary schools has meant a surge in the production of good quality software that may be used in Key Stage 1 mathematics. Multiplication tables testers have been around for a while and certainly vary in quality but a good one can motivate children, record their results, recognise weaknesses and set up individually designed tests. Data handling packages are numerous and can be very helpful when used with individuals or small groups (Exchanging and Sharing Information). Some programs enable good work with symmetry with the children designing a picture and the program reflecting it in any number of ways. The Internet hosts dozens of sites that contain mathematical materials. Care needs to be taken with some sites because they can come and go quite quickly (Finding Things Out). The last thing needed is for a precious site to go down just before the Ofsted inspector arrives.

History

The links are not strong but timelines are a useful way of presenting information in a way that shows order. Although the numbers involved (for example, the date of the Great Fire of London) may be difficult at Key Stage 1, recognition of the numbers (for example, dates) being ordered is important (Chronological Understanding). There are also very good opportunities for using the language of comparison, for example, 'long ago', 'ages' and 'recent'.

PE and Games

Work on position and direction fit neatly into PE schemes. Simple games such as Duck, Duck, Goose encourage mathematics and listening skills. Having children work in groups can provide lots of good mathematical vocabulary opportunities; for example, ask them to move into groups of two, three, four. Fractions can take on meaning if you split the class into two, three of four groups. The language of comparison can be promoted heavily; for example, 'move a little closer to the mat', 'jump a bit higher', 'who is next?'.

Links with other subjects

Design and Technology/Art and Design

Pattern often comes into the design part of these subjects (Knowledge and Understanding). If the children are studying weaving, the patterns they think of should be considered in a mathematical way. The idea of patterns being attractive come into both subjects (Evaluating and Developing Work). Accurate measurement and drawing is very important to Technology and children should be expected to use a full range of instruments correctly, measuring to the nearest centimetre at least (Working with Tools, Equipment, Materials and Components to Make Quality Products).

Music

Once again work with patterns is a natural part of this subject (Creating and Developing Musical Ideas – Composing Skills). The children may be asked to play either in groups or individually but while considering the timing and duration (Listening and Applying Knowledge and Understanding). Working with the note lengths involves fractions.

Note: parentheses indicate references to *The National Curriculum – Handbook for primary teachers in England* (1999)

Counting

Within Number, counting is widely considered to be the most important aspect of early mathematical work in Key Stage 1. Apart from the obvious 'real life' benefits of being able to count accurately, a good knowledge of counting and a recognition of how numbers can be linked together through counting on or counting back, leads to the early understanding of addition, subtraction, multiplication and division. Through this work, other important maths elements are introduced. These include odd and even and the idea of multiples.

For the young child, it is very important to show that counting has practical applications. In this way they come to see maths as a useful tool, not an enemy language which is meaningless. It is better to ask children 'How many children are in front of you in the dinner queue?' than 'What is 7 add 8?'. Teachers should always try to make the counting as real as possible. Although this cannot always be the case, interesting displays and colourful illustrations of number based work does help.

Very young children should also be encouraged to begin estimating when carrying out early work in counting groups of up to ten or 100 objects. Estimation should not be underestimated as a skill. Children need to be told that an estimate is a clever guess. Through practice and a widening knowledge of number, an estimate can become a very clever guess.

Recording skills are also introduced at this very early stage. Clearly, this will be very difficult for some Year 1 children and they will need assistance.

That does not mean they should not try. The recording of the thought process – the method – is becoming more important as the standards of mathematics in the primary years rises. This is because basic computational skills are now being carried out fairly successfully and the need exists to have children look deeper into how they are achieving an answer. This means they will need to examine their own thinking process.

Putting thoughts into words is difficult for children, especially the very young but the earlier the opportunities the better. The recording does not need to be complicated. If a Year 2 child has counted in steps of five from 15 to 30 they could say: 'I put my finger on 15, counted five along to 20, counted five along to 25, counted five along to 30. I moved my finger three lots of five times.' It is likely that a word bank for maths terms will be needed. It is likely that Year 1 children will sometimes need a scribe.

Knowing the number names and being able to match those to the symbols is very important. Along with this goes the gradual learning of the sequence of the numbers. If this work takes place as explicit lessons and through 'drip feeding' opportunities, it makes the actual counting process much easier.

Counting on and back from various starting points is very important but be careful about rushing into taking this one step further into addition and subtraction. The importance of counting on and back in fixed steps is to enable exploration of the number system to about 100, not manipulating the numbers through calculations.

Number names to 20

Learning outcome

To know the number names and recite them to and from at least 20 (Y1)

Assumed knowledge and experience

Most children will have heard many number names being used on a daily basis. They will also be used to seeing numbers all around them in a wide range of contexts. Much of this knowledge will have come from opportunities to hear simple rhymes or counting songs, for example, 'One, Two, Three, Four, Five, Once I Caught a Fish Alive' or 'Ten in a Bed'.

Mathematical importance

Children must be able to recognise the names of the numbers so that they can later link the names to the actual amounts. On some occasions these links will happen simultaneously, especially with the smaller numbers such as 1–4. Being able to recite the number names in the correct order helps to internalise the sequence, which relates to the amounts.

Activities

Use a few minutes to have the children tell you the names of some rhyming poems or counting verses they may know. After a short while, narrow the children down to naming verses and poems which contain numbers. The titles might be written down. Expect answers to include 'Three Blind Mice', 'This Old Man'. Choose a couple of poems or verses to say as a class or by the individual who named it. Highlight the fact that in the examples given, the numbers follow in order and ask them to think about saying the numbers in order beginning from 1. This can lead into reciting the numbers to 10 and beyond. It may be that some children will already be able to undertake this work in which case they might work with a classroom assistant going on to higher numbers. Try to break the 'tens barriers' and reach at least 12 with confidence before taking the whole class on towards 20.

During follow-on sessions, make reciting games to 20 part of the culture. Have girls begin from 1, then alternate with boys saying the next number. This will also introduce the idea of odds and evens although this will probably not be made explicit.

Spend some time discussing the children's birthdays. Once these have been established, possibly using the register, arrange the children in order according to the numbers.

Towards the end of the work, the children should be able to recite a sequence starting from a number other than 1. If homework is set, the children may be asked to find the birthdays of friends and relatives and arrange them in order. They might try to remember the names that go with a date number and tell the class about what they find out.

Points to watch

Numbers in the wrong order. Numbers omitted when reciting. Numbers being repeated.

Resources

Big Books, especially those which contain rhymes, which will include number names; pictures of the numbers with their names displayed around the classroom; a puppet or 'speaking toy' which can recite the numbers – rightly and wrongly; tapes of counting rhymes and tape player

Next step

Know the number names beyond 20, possibly to 31. Recite the numbers with confidence. Be able to say the next number after a given number and the one before it.

Number names to 31

Learning outcome

Know the number names and recite them to and from 31 (Y1)

Assumed knowledge and experience

The children should by now have a fairly firm grasp of the numbers up to 20. They should be able to recite them with some confidence and at least say the next number. Some, possibly most, should be able to say the previous number. The children should also have become used to seeing the number names and number forms in the classroom around them.

Mathematical importance

Most children are fairly familiar with number names up to about 20. This will vary greatly between children but 20 is often considered a level of knowledge which may also match their conceptual ability to visualise and internalise a number. Taking the number names to 31 is the next step. Thirty-one has been selected for two reasons. Firstly, it crosses the 29/30 border and shows the sequence of numbers continuing in a simple recognisable pattern. Secondly, it is the maximum number of days in a month and, as such, still contains many number names, which the children will be familiar with.

Activities

The children should be used to constant practice using the numbers and number names to 20. Begin by asking them what they think happens beyond 20. Is 20 the last number or are their others? Ask the children to name some other numbers they either know or can imagine. Write these on the board. If individual whiteboards are being used, have each child write down a few 'new' numbers. Select a few of the children's numbers for discussion. Without going into any depth about tens and units, ask the children what they know about the numbers. The answers will vary greatly; some children may want to talk about 'bigger than' or 'smaller than'. These children should be congratulated but the focus must not be diverted from the main theme 'What happens after 20?'.

After some discussion, reveal a group of objects which have been hidden from view until now. The more interesting the objects the better but they should all be the same for the sake of simplicity – counters would do if nothing else were available. Have the objects arranged in some simple array, possibly four rows of five. The children now count out loud the number of objects as the array is moved

sequentially around. Twenty objects will be seen. Add one more object. Ask the children how many objects there are now. It may be necessary to say 'twenty and one' to begin with and then point out that this is easier said as 'twenty-one'. Add another object and ask what this amount might be called. Continue until 29. Children will usually be comfortable up to 29 without too much trouble but be warned, knowing the names of the numbers does not mean the children have an understanding of the amount they represent at this stage. After 29, add one more object and ask what this amount will be. Some children may say 'twenty ten'. It may well be necessary to tell the children that we call this new number 'thirty' and that after the 'tens' numbers and the 'twenties' numbers we have the 'thirties' numbers. This can be a difficult step for some and reinforcement will often be needed. Once the 29/30 barrier has been crossed, finish by adding one more to see who can pick up that this might be called 'thirty-one'.

Many infant classes have a maximum of 30 children and if the teacher is included, the total is 31. This fact can be well used in counting exercises.

Points to watch

The children who concentrate so hard on saying the 'twenty' that they forget which unit number is next. Children who are failing to grasp that 30 follows 29.

Resources

Interesting objects but the less able children will be confused by twenty different objects, especially if

they vary greatly in size; counters but small coloured teddy bears – sometimes used for baseline assessments – would be better

Next step

The next step in naming the numbers is up to 100 in Year 2. This work should go alongside work that gives meaning to the amounts represented by the names and is not an end in itself.

Number names to 100

Learning outcome

To say the number names in order to at least 100, from and back to 0 (Y2)

Assumed knowledge and experience

The children should have been working with number and the number names for some time and be familiar with the numbers and, to a degree, their values, up to 31 at least. In general terms, they will be aware of larger numbers and many will talk about numbers such as 50 or hundreds.

Mathematical importance

The move from knowledge of 20 or 31 to 100 is part of the process through which children come to understand about numbers and the way in which they grow. For many children the pattern of the growth to 99 is straightforward although remembering the actual number names needs practice. The jump to 100 is very significant.

Activities

Arrange the multiples of 10 from 20 to 90 vertically on an OHP transparency with the 20 revealed but the other numbers covered. Have the children recite from 0 to 20 and when they reach 20 stop them. Ask them about what comes next and they should be able to recite readily from 21 to 30. Stop them at 30 and reveal the number on the OHP. Ask again what comes next.

They should continue to 39 and some may be hesitant about the next number. Reveal the 40 and tell them that we call this number 'forty'. At this point, reveal all of the tens numbers to 90. Tell the children the names of the tens numbers and have them repeat them in various ways, for example, according to the numbers of boys/girls/houses. After practice of just the tens, ask what comes after 40 and most will realise 41. Go to 50 and repeat the process. Continue in this way to 99.

It may be necessary to undertake this activity in at least two sessions, probably more. When some confidence has been achieved to 99, tell the children that the next number is very special and ask if anyone can guess what its name is. After a little time that might generate the correct answer, tell them it is 100.

Make all the children repeat the name and repeat the sequence from 90 to 100 a number of times. Depending on the ability of the children, it is likely that this activity will need to be repeated many times.

Once some knowledge has been built up, reinforce the number names to 100 by using a number line or number square. Number squares might be photocopied for each child or they could use published magnetic number squares to go with individual whiteboards.

Many children will pick up the number names to 100 fairly quickly and it may be possible to use classroom assistants to give support to the less confident. It is worth noting that although, place value is clearly part of this work, it does not need to be taught explicitly.

Practise reciting the tens numbers back and forth to 100, and beyond if appropriate, at odd times during the day, for example, while waiting for assembly.

Look for opportunities during the year to collect numbers to 100. These could be birthdays, amounts of money, home address. Begin the children counting on from any point and then reciting backwards from 100 to 0.

Point to watch

Children who continually forget the sequence of the tens multiples.

Resources

OHP and transparencies; individual whiteboards and felt-tips; number line to 100 marked in tens only; number line to 100 marked with all units; number squares

Next step

Read and write whole numbers to at least 1000 (Y3).

Counting to 20/31

Learning outcome

To count reliably to at least 20 and then 31 (Y1)

Assumed knowledge and experience

By Year 1, most children will have some understanding of counting although it may not have been explicit. Most children can count to five simply through experiences at home; for example, 'How many fish fingers would you like?'. Children will be learning about the number names at the same time (see pages 2 and 3).

Mathematical importance

The children must come to realise that the last number in the count gives the size of the group. They must also understand that counting is a mathematical skill, which is very useful and will always be important to them. Although counting is often done from left to right, children must be able to count random groups, for example, five fish in a goldfish bowl.

Activities

The counting experiences should be as realistic as possible. Small coloured cubes may be freely available but will not make for an exciting lesson. Try Smarties! Place a packet (not a tube) of Smarties on each table and have the children open the box on to a clean napkin. After discussion of favourite colours, have the children count the Smarties but without touching them! Encourage the children to record the number. Now move quickly between the groups and make a big show of jiggling the napkin around and thus redistributing the Smarties. Ask the children to count again. Many will understand that the number has not changed but others will not and it is a useful opportunity to reinforce the idea of conservation of number. Have the children record the second count. Go around the groups and ask for results. Have they counted accurately? Have results changed? Now let the children share the Smarties if you wish but check for allergies beforehand.

Now use an OHP and place randomly on the screen various easily available objects, for example, erasers or pencils. Have the children silently count the objects (up to twenty). Record the result. Remove some objects and have them count again. Repeat this a number of times, recording the results each time. Return the original number of objects and ask for results. Discuss the results and, when disagreements arise, have children come to the OHP and count using their finger to point.

Have a range of objects available – cubes may be easiest to find. Put a tub of cubes on each table. Have each child write down a number between 5 and 31. This can be differentiated according to ability. Now have each child collect the correct number of cubes and place these in front of them. Have another child count the objects to see if they match the written number. The classroom assistant may be needed for the less able children. Put the cubes back in the tub and have each child give a friend a 'target' number. Repeat the counting game.

Have displays of small objects around the room. On a daily basis, add to or subtract from these groups and send groups or individuals off to count them.

Points to watch

Accurate attempts at counting but failure to know the number names. Inaccurate counting – help by arranging in rows and insisting on counting from left to right.

Resources

Boxes of Smarties, beads, counters, cubes, leaves, pencils, erasers, nuts; OHP

Next step

Count reliably to at least 100 (Y2). This will need to be done in stages alongside the number name development.

Counting to 100

Learning outcome

To count reliably up to 100 objects by grouping (Y2)

Assumed knowledge and experience

The children should have had many opportunities to count to at least 31 and have a developing knowledge of the number names to 100 (see page 3). They should have an understanding that larger numbers than 20 and 31 exist and have some experience of seeing the numbers in written form at home, in the environment and at school.

Mathematical importance

Counting accurately is an important life skill. The opportunity to count as high as 100 also gives the first chance to develop the idea of estimation. Counting large amounts by grouping is also introduced at this level.

Activities

This activity will require the multilink-type cubes which can be joined together. Place a large number of small cubes on the OHP and ask the children to estimate how many are there. It is important to tell the children from the beginning that an estimate is a 'clever guess'. If individual whiteboards are available, have the children write their estimates on them and when asked, show them to the rest of the class. Ensure that all children write numbers and not words such as 'lots' or 'hundreds'. It is most likely that the estimates will vary widely so write some examples on the board to illustrate this fact.

Now ask the children if they can think of any ways to make an accurate count. They are likely to suggest counting individual cubes and it may be necessary to ask 'Will that be easy?'. Hopefully, someone might suggest the possibility that you might lose count! You may need to suggest that separating the cubes into smaller groups would be helpful. Once this is established, ask what the best size of group might be. For our purposes, we will use groups of ten. The least able children may be given cubes up to about 50 (48, for example) and, with the help of a classroom assistant, they can group them into tens and make them into 'sticks'. They may need support to

translate the four sticks and eight singles into the number name 48. The main group should be given cubes up to 100 (84, for example) and told to make tens sticks out of them and record the result as a proper number, for example, not eight sticks and four or eight tens and four but 84.

Clearly place value is important and may be discussed but the focus of this activity is counting by grouping. Set strict time limits for each count and then jumble up the cubes and start another grouping and counting opportunity. The most able children might want to try grouping in other ways or using tally charts. Working in pairs, one child could count out ten while the other keeps a tally. The roles can be reversed the next time. All the children may want to consider how to group for smaller or larger numbers. It might be more appropriate to group in twos if numbers up to 20 are being counted, for example.

Complete the work by having the children compare their grouped count with their estimate. This is most important. The more able children may want to keep a record of their estimate and the actual result, then work out, possibly using a calculator, if they are becoming more accurate.

Points to watch

Accurate counting for the tens sticks. Have the children place the sticks alongside each other so that incorrect amounts become obvious.

Resources

Linking cubes

Next step

Counting larger collections by grouping them in different ways (Y3).

Counting in ones/tens and hundreds

Learning outcome

To count on and back in ones from any small number (Y1)

To count on and back in tens and hundreds from and back to 0 (Y1)

Assumed knowledge and experience

Children should have a fairly secure knowledge of the number names and be able to recite them backwards and forwards with some confidence. The number names for the multiples of 10 to at least 100 should be known.

Mathematical importance

This work bridges the gap between knowing the number names and being able to recite them, and the beginnings of addition and subtraction. Through counting on and counting back activities, the children will come to see that numbers can become smaller or greater depending upon what is done to them.

Activities

Number lines, which can be written on, are very useful for counting on and back. To begin with, draw a simple number line on a board. Make the spaces for each number obvious, squares are best. Put a 0 in the first square and then ask the whole class to count on one. It is most important that the children understand what is meant by 'counting on'. As they say the next number, write it down. This simple exercise will help the children become used to the phrase 'counting on' and give them a little confidence because of its ease.

After a while, draw a new blank number line but this time enter a number other than 0 in the first place. Have the children count on in ones from that number. Repeat a few times, each time starting with a higher number, depending upon the ability of the children.

Now repeat the same task but using the phrase 'counting back' or simple variations, for example, 'count backwards'. If the children are ready to move on, hand out prepared activity sheets that contain number lines with some numbers already placed on them. A simple instruction such as 'count on four' should enable the children to begin work.

They will simply complete the lines as requested in the instructions.

A similar process can be worked through with counting in tens to 100. A large number square is useful for this activity (see page 88 in *Blueprints Maths Key Stage 1: Pupil Resource Book*). Start by counting on and back using the multiples of 10. After a short while, make the task more difficult by counting on from any number, for example, in tens from 17 or back in tens from 91. This work is invaluable in building up a firm knowledge of the numbers to 100 and how they are related. The main group and the more able children can be asked to count on three lots of tens or back two lots of tens as examples of more challenging questions.

Sit the children in a circle. Choose a counting on or back activity with ones or tens. Give a child in the group a starting number and have each child say the next number in the sequence.

Points to watch

Counting in hundreds needs to be dealt with carefully in Year 1 but children are usually interested in how numbers grow and it is worth discussing 'What comes one after 100?' and 'What hundred-number comes after 100?'.

Resources

Large number square marked to 100; prepared number lines; blank number lines for use with children who need more challenge during the activities

Next steps

Counting on and back from two-digit numbers as confidence increases. Counting on in twos from 1 and 0.

Counting from any two-digit number

Learning outcome

To count on or back in ones and tens, starting from any two-digit number (Y2)

Assumed knowledge and experience

The children should have a good knowledge of the number names from 0 to 100 and a growing experience of phrases like 'counting on' and 'counting back'. They should have confidence in recognising larger numbers and in saying the names quickly.

Mathematical importance

This work takes the child's knowledge of number forward by giving them the ability to count on and back to and from two-digit numbers and thus build the foundations for addition and subtraction. It also gives an opportunity for recording mathematics in sentence form.

Activities

Counting in ones and tens continues the work started earlier in Year 2 (see page 7). The children should now be ready for more thought provoking questions that are entering the realms of addition and subtraction. It is likely that these words will be used concurrently with counting on and counting back and some teachers may feel it appropriate to begin using symbols.

Give a 1–100 number square to each child. Explain that they must choose any number they like as a starting point and colour it in. Then, for example, tell all the children to count on six from that number and colour in the result. Then change colour and tell the children to choose a different starting number. Continue five or six times. Have a few children show their squares to the rest of the class. If whiteboards are available, give all the children the same starting number and give them instructions, such as 'count back eight' or 'count on seven from 19'.

Eventually the children should be able to count in ones and tens without the aid of number squares and lines. Differentiated questions will need to be used but children should be asked to do such things as: count on in tens from 46 to 86; count back from 70 to 10 (how many tens did you count?); count back nine from 61; describe this pattern, 45, 55, 65 (what are the next three numbers?).

When confidence has grown, have each child compile a small booklet or record of 'My Counting Facts'. Each child can use a number square or number line to help illustrate some facts they have discovered. They should be encouraged to write their facts in proper sentences wherever possible and use correct mathematical language. Sentences might be: 'I counted on seven from 5 and the answer was 12', 'If you count backwards in tens from 43, you get to 3', 'Thirty is four lots of 10 away from 70.'

Points to watch

None

Resources

Whiteboards; 1–100 number squares

Next step

Counting on beyond the 100 border. Working differences between numbers such as 53 and 83 (Y3).

Counting in twos

Learning outcome

To count on in twos from 0, then 1 (Y1)

To count on in twos from and back to 0 or any small number (Y2)

Assumed knowledge and experience

The children should have an understanding of phrases such as 'counting on' and 'counting back'. They should have a knowledge of number names and the correct sequence to at least 31 (Y1) and 100 (Y2).

Mathematical importance

Counting on in twos is an important step in beginning to understand odds and evens. Working with twos will also lead into multiplication tables and use of multiples.

Activities

Year 1

Counting in twos is helped by a number line. With the whole class, point to 0 and then tell the children to count on two and tell you the number they have arrived on. Mark the number with a felt-tip. Continue counting on in twos until 10 is reached, marking the numbers as you go. Ask the children if they have noticed a pattern yet. They should use words and phrases like 'skipped over', 'jumped', 'missed out' or 'every other one'. Make sure they all realise that when counting in twos, the pattern of 'every other one' always applies. Once this has been established, ask the children to predict what the next number will be without counting on. Most should say 12. Continue up to 20. Now repeat but starting from 1 and going to 21.

Once the exercise has been completed, make a listing of the 'two jumps' which started from 0 and those which started from 1. Ask the children if they can say which numbers come next in this more abstract format. Some may mention odds and evens.

Odds and evens should be handled with care. The children should be given small numbers of objects such as counters. Ask the children to share them equally between two. Those numbers which can be shared equally, for example, 2, 4, 6, 8, 10, are even

numbers. Those numbers which have an odd one left over are called odd numbers. The children need to have this explained carefully. Give out up to twenty counters and repeat the exercise. As this work progresses, a list should be compiled of the odd and even numbers to 20. Emphasise that even numbers or amounts can be shared equally by two but odd numbers cannot be shared equally by two.

Year 2

The children's knowledge of odds and evens needs to be consolidated. Have the children count in twos starting from 0. They should be able to count easily beyond 40. Now start from 1 and do the same thing. Now have them begin at a number between 0 and 40 and count backwards in twos. Repeat as often as possible using different starting numbers.

The children may be given a number square up to 50. Have them start at 0 and circle every other number. Now start at 1 and cross through every other number. Do they notice a pattern? Give a label to each child with a random number from 0 to 50. Have the children separate into odd and even groups according to their labels. Swap the labels and repeat. The children can recite the numbers from 0, clapping once for the odd numbers and twice when even numbers are said.

Points to watch

Children starting to recognise that odd and even numbers always end in the same set of digits. The less able children who may be confident to 8 or 10 but have not grasped the concept.

Resources

Number lines; counters or cubes for sharing; labels; number squares to 50

Next step

To recognise odd and even numbers in mathematical and 'real life' situations (Y2).

Odds and evens

Learning outcome

To begin to recognise odd and even numbers to at least 20 (Y1)

To recognise odd and even numbers beyond 20 (Y2)

Assumed knowledge and experience

The children should have a basic understanding of odd and even. They should have undertaken pencil and paper exercises and reciting work to give them a good awareness of odds and evens to about 40.

They should be familiar with counting on and back in twos from different starting numbers.

Mathematical importance

Understanding odds and evens relates to the way mathematicians view numbers. Numbers are interesting and many are special for different reasons. Odds and evens are early examples of this. Later the children will generalise about ways of recognising odd and even numbers however large they may be.

Activities

The children need plenty of activities that will help them to recognise odd and even numbers in the school, home and environment.

Have Year 1 children make a small 'Odds and Evens' book. This does not need to be large but will contain information the children have discovered. The following suggestions could be the basis for the contents and all relate to recognising odds and evens:

Number of children in the class

Number of boys/girls in the class

Number of children sitting at the desk

Number of teachers in the school

Number of black/white/grey socks worn in my class

Number of tables in the room

Number in my family

Number of my house

Place a 1–50 square or line on the board and every time a child finds a fact for that number, place a tick

on it thus building up a simple display. Make sure all the numbers are addressed at least once.

Year 2 children should recognise certain facts about odds and evens. They should be able to say that all even numbers divide exactly by two and that there is always one left over – 'odd' – when an odd number is divided by two.

Give the children, either individually or in groups, selections of numbers and have them sort them into odds and evens. The size of the numbers may be differentiated for ability groups. Less able children may be given cubes or counters to help them. The main group and the more able children can be asked more challenging questions, such as 'What is the next odd number after 23?', 'Which even number comes between 30 and 34?' or 'Name the two odd numbers before 42'. Use Activity sheet 9. The more able children could be asked to sort the numbers 30, 39, 46, 61, 77 and 93 after they have sorted the numbers 1–24.

Some children may be able to use the memory button on a calculator to continually add on two. This is a legitimate use of a calculator that will be particularly challenging to able children.

Points to watch

Children who have difficulty with continuing sequences of odd and even when starting in positions other than 0 or 1. Children who have memorised the odds and evens to about 10 but then have little idea about what is meant.

Resources

Cubes; counters; small booklet/pamphlet of blank paper

Next step

Making general statements about odds and evens and recognising the effect of adding odds and evens in different ways (Y3).

Steps of five and three

Learning outcome

To count in steps of five from 0 to at least 20, then back again (Y1)

To begin to count on in steps of three from 0 (Y1)

Assumed knowledge and experience

The children should be familiar with the number names to at least 31 and have a good understanding of 'counting on' and 'counting back' and simple variants on those phrases. They should recognise from counting in twos (see pages 9 and 10) that counting on in set steps will produce patterns.

Mathematical importance

Through work on counting in steps of two, the children will be starting to develop a mathematical idea of patterns and simple ways in which they develop. Counting in steps of five and then three helps take counting skills forward as well as giving opportunities for remembering the number names and sequence. Addition and subtraction with small numbers is also part of this work although not explicitly. It also opens the way to 5× and 3× tables and working with multiples.

Activities

Begin with a number line that extends from 0 to at least 20. Warm up with the children counting to and from 20 in ones, then twos. Repeat but with the number line covered. Tell the children that they will be counting in even bigger steps today – steps of five. Begin from 0 and have each child count on five. Individual whiteboards would be useful so that each child can write down their 'answer'. Hear a few answers and correct any errors. Move on to the next five-step and repeat until 20 is reached. Mark the 'five' numbers in an obvious way. Make a separate list of the 'five' numbers and ask if anyone can predict what will come next. Practise reciting the 'five' numbers whenever possible. Give the children a chance to recite them from 20 back to 0.

Give each child in the class a number card up to the total number of the children, for example, 30. Have the children order themselves into a line or a circle. Ask all of the children to think who has the 'five' numbers, including 0. You then call 'Stand up' and the children call out the name of whoever has 0. Repeat in order up to the highest 'five' number. Swap all the numbers around and repeat as often as you like.

Put counters or cubes on each table. Ask each child to make five piles of five objects. When all are ready, have the children say out loud 'Five, ten, fifteen, twenty, twenty-five' as they touch each pile without knocking them down. Repeat from 25 back down.

For steps of three, use a number line again. Give each child a number line from 0 to 30. Have all the children colour in 0 and count on in steps of three. Have the main group and the more able children also put a tick above the even numbers. Have an assistant work with the less able group making sure all is being done correctly, while the results of the rest of the class are taken forward. Ask them to recite the 'three step' numbers they have coloured. Ask which numbers are coloured in and also have a tick. Make a list of these numbers and ask if anyone can see how big their 'jump' is. Have the children try to memorise the sequence 0, 3, 6, 9, 12, 15, 18.

Points to watch

Many children will spot that all '5' numbers will either end in 0 or 5. The less able will have difficulty counting on five and are likely to count on three or four instead.

Resources

Counters; cubes; number line to at least 20

Next step

Counting on in steps of three, four and five beyond 20 and back to any small number (Y2).

Steps of three, four and five

Learning outcome

To count in steps of three, four and five to at least 30 from and back to 0 and any small number (Y2)

Assumed knowledge and experience

The children should have a very good knowledge of the number names to at least 100. They should also understand the sequence of the numbers and be able to count forward and backwards in ones and tens with confidence. Considerable experience with counting in steps of two should have taken place and some experience in counting in steps of three and five would be useful.

Mathematical importance

Counting in steps with these numbers helps to build an understanding of numbers and addition and subtraction skills, although this may not be explicit during the work. It also lays the foundations for the 2×, 3×, 4×, 5× and 10× tables.

Activities

Give each child an activity sheet containing a number square marked from 1 to 100 and rows of five 'empty' stars. The children begin by selecting any number from the number square and colouring it in. They write this number in the first star in the top row. Next they fill in the numbers in the remainder of the row which will be equivalent to counting on five, one at a time. Finally they should fill in the end 'star' number on the number square in the same colour as the starting number. Repeat the process, using a different colour or pattern with each new starting and finishing number.

This work can easily be varied to allow for counting in different steps, to and from.

Counting in steps of four may not have been encountered before. Using a number line, have the children count on and back in steps of two several times. Now have them count on and back from 0 in steps of four, marking the numbers as you go. Do this a few times. Compile a separate list on the board of the 'four' numbers. Have the children recite the 'four' numbers. Ask if they can predict the next numbers.

Use a number line to see if the children see a connection between the numbers in the 'two' sequence and those in the 'four'.

The children have usually worked with counting starting from 0 or 1. Now the foundations have been laid, they need to move forward and be able to count on and back in steps of one, two, three, four, five and ten to and from any small number.

With assistance, if possible, for the less able children, give the children simple tasks that require them to record their results. Individual whiteboards would be very useful. This work is deliberately done in abstract for the main and more able groups. Give the children a series of tasks such as: beginning from 2, count on four; starting from 21, count back three; count on five from 66; what number comes next? 15, 18, 21.

It is important that the questions are put in lots of different ways so that the children become used to discovering and dealing with the problem. Answers can be written on the whiteboards and shown to you. This work can be followed up with plenty of opportunities to practise on paper.

Points to watch

This is a critical stage of development. Children who are not coping with the general concept of counting, need to be given plenty of opportunities and use a wide variety of formats.

Resources

Number lines; counters; individual whiteboards

Next step

Beginning formal addition and subtraction and starting to look at multiples.

Multiples of 2, 5 and 10

Learning outcome

To begin to recognise multiples of 2, 5 and 10 (Y2)

Assumed knowledge and experience

The children should have had many opportunities to count on and back in two, five and ten. They should be familiar with the numbers, which are in the two, five and ten sequences when starting from 0. Some hints have been given in earlier work that ways of spotting multiples of 2, 5 and 10 exist!

Mathematical importance

Multiples are another way in which mathematicians group or classify numbers. They connect strongly with multiplication and division work that will follow later.

Activities

Begin with the numbers in the ten sequence when counting on from 0. Ask the children to name these numbers and write them on the board as they do. Going a little way beyond 100 would be fine. Tell the children that numbers that can be divided exactly by a smaller number are called multiples of that number and that these numbers are all multiples of 10. Make sure the correct term is used and is written clearly on a board. Ask if they notice something similar about the numbers. The response that they all end in 0 should be straightforward. Ask if they think all multiples of 10 end in 0 and discuss this with any children who disagree.

Now ask them to give the five-number sequence as far as they can. Only write up to about 30 or 40 on the board to save time. Can they now see a way of telling if a number is a multiple of 5 by just looking at it? They should spot that all multiples of 5 end in either 5 or 0. Ask if any numbers are multiples of 5 and 10. Now progress to the two sequence and write up to 30 or 40 on the board. Is there an easy way to spot multiples of 2? Discuss this with the children. Which numbers are multiples of 2, 5 and 10 all at once?

Number squares are a good means of reinforcing the multiples. Have the children tick the multiples of 2 on a 1–100 number square. Please note that actually colouring them all in is a bit of a waste of time. Can they spot a pattern? Have them describe the pattern verbally and in writing. Repeat with the 5 and the 10. Make sure they describe the pattern.

Use an activity sheet that shows a group of numbers, most of which are multiples of 2, 5 or 10. Tell the children to circle the multiples of 2 in red, multiples of 5 in green and multiples of 10 in blue. If numbers are multiples of more than one of these, they should be coloured in the appropriate colours. A few numbers should not be multiples and these can act as a 'trap' for those who are unsure. Numbers could be 15, 8, 30, 21, 60, 85, 3, for example.

The main group and more able children should be given larger numbers, perhaps beyond 100, for example, 115 or 162, and asked what they are multiples of.

Points to watch

Some children will think that simply counting on two, five or ten from any number will generate another multiple of that number. This is not so and it needs to be made explicit that a multiple is a number which can be divided or shared exactly.

Resources

Colouring pencils; 1–100 number squares; activity sheet

Next step

Multiples of numbers ending in 00. Multiples of 2, 5 and 10 beyond 100.

Place value

An understanding of place value is considered an essential prerequisite to developing a good knowledge of number and ways of working with number. Although as adults we use the term 'place', children often find the word 'position' easier to understand and teachers often explain to children that the position of a particular digit in a number is important rather than the 'place'. It is important for children to know that they mean the same thing.

The sequence with place value should be straightforward, moving from single digits, through two-digit numbers, three-digit numbers and so on. Inevitably some children will have heard of hundreds, thousands and millions and this knowledge, and probable interest, should be used as a positive factor in gradually discovering what comes next!

Great care must be taken to ensure that the understanding at each stage of the sequence is secure. A surprising number of children do not realise that in this context T stands for tens and U stands for units. Although many children may be able to 'read' the number 37 as thirty-seven, when asked what the value of the '3' is, they often do not know. Failure to understand the importance of the positional value leads to poor understanding of addition and subtraction and the skills of estimation and approximation become almost impossible.

Partitioning of numbers into their constituent parts has regained some importance because of the National Numeracy Strategy. Most teachers have always used the idea of partitioning but it has been given more explicit emphasis recently. Children should be encouraged to partition numbers and understand what it means. They should be able to use partition and partitioning as natural parts of their developing mathematical vocabulary.

Read and write numbers 20/100

Learning outcome

To read and write numerals from 0 to at least 20 (Y1)

To read and write whole numbers to at least 100 in figures and words (Y2)

Assumed knowledge and experience

This work is closely linked with very early work on knowing the number names. It is likely to run alongside it (see pages 2–4) and should not be seen as separate in any way. The children should be able to recognise some numerals from their environment and from work in the Foundation stage. This ability will vary widely.

Mathematical importance

Children need to be able to see the shape of a number and 'read' what it says; for example, 9 says nine. This is different from being able to say the number names in the context of something like a nursery rhyme. Young children need to be able to 'put a name to the face'. After 9, the importance of the position of each digit becomes very important.

Activities

Prepare three or four sets of large number cards with the numerals 0 to 9 shown clearly. Distribute these at random to the class and have the children sit in a circle. Place the cards in clear view in front of each child. A series of questions needs to be given which will help the children learn to match words with pictures: 'Who has the number 3?', 'Emma's card says 9. What does Darius's card say?', 'Pedro, say the name of your card'. Once confidence has been built to 9, move on to 20.

Prepare sets of cards, which show up to nine spots. The spots are best arranged in simple patterns as if on a dice face. Distribute these to the children and continue in a similar vein to that above: 'Whose cards show eight spots?', 'Which cards show three spots?'. Swap the cards and repeat often.

Simple bingo cards can be produced with the numbers just going up to 20. Distribute the cards and play bingo in the traditional way.

If individual whiteboards are available to the whole class or to a group, say various numbers and have the children write them down in figures. The children hold up the boards to show their answers and a quick response can be given.

By the end of Year 1, most children should be able to write the figures 1–20 and some will also be able to write them in words.

As the children progress to Year 2, the exercises can remain similar although the numbers should reach 100. A number square or line is easier to use than homemade cards. Magnetic 1–100 number squares can be bought to use individually with small whiteboards. If a class square is being used, point to various numbers and ask children to tell you the name. Say the name of a number and ask children to point to that number. This is more easily and productively done with small squares where you can say 'Colour in 78 blue, colour in 39 red', for example.

Points to watch

Children reversing numbers either when writing or reading them; for example, saying 23 as 'thirty-two'.

Resources

Sets of number cards 0–9; sets of numbers showing spots 0–9; 1–100 number square; bingo cards; individual whiteboards

Next step

Begin to understand that the position (place) of a numeral is very important (Y1 and Y2).

Partitioning

Learning outcome

To begin to know what each digit in a two-digit number represents (Y1)

To begin to understand the partition of 'teens' numbers (Y1)

Assumed knowledge and experience

A knowledge of the number names up to at least 20 is expected and they should have counting experiences with at least twenty objects.

Mathematical importance

Working with numbers can be difficult and confusing but mathematicians try to make things as simple as possible. One of the main ways is by giving importance to the position of digits in numbers larger than 9. We know by the position (place), the value a digit has. Children must learn that this importance of position (place value) is central to understanding and using numbers.

Activities

Linking cubes will be very useful in this activity but non-linking cubes will do. The children should sit around in a circle while you put 23 cubes into the centre as one pile. Begin by asking the children to estimate how many cubes there might be. Write some of the estimates on the board. Now ask what might be the best way to count them accurately. After a chance for discussion, arrange the cubes into a long row – not joined. Ask if this is easier to count. Suggest that the line is a bit long and that it would be helpful if we could break the line into smaller bits. Tell the children that we use 10 as a useful amount for the smaller bits. You might remind them that we have ten fingers, so 10 is a useful number.

Have a child count out ten cubes and join them together. Have a second child count out another ten and a third child count out what is left. Arrange the two tens next to each other with the three units alongside. At this early stage, ensure that correct mathematical vocabulary is used. Tell the children that we call the sticks of cubes 'tens' and the others 'units'. Write '2 tens' and '3 units' on the board, then tell the children that we do not need to write 'tens' and 'units', we just write 23. Discuss whose estimate was the closest.

This activity should be gone through as many times as possible but it is important that, every time a new collection of cubes is counted, you model on the board the method of presenting the answer. Please note that more than twenty cubes have been used in this example because it helps the idea of dividing into groups of ten, more than the 'teens' numbers would.

Give out twenty cubes between two children. Have one child remove a small number of cubes, then both of them make a tens stick and the units out of the rest. They should then record the result in their book. Repeat several times. The children are likely to 'test the limits' a bit and start to remove ever larger numbers of cubes. When more than ten is removed, tell them to record the larger amount. This work can give the more able children some real thinking to do about subtraction.

This should not become a time wasting exercise where the children spend more time drawing tiny squares than they do counting and thinking about place value. Within reason, it is perfectly all right for children to quickly draw the outline of a tens stick and the units without being terribly accurate. They could also draw around the tens stick. Use of a traditional abacus might be appropriate with some children after practice with this exercise.

Points to watch

Reversing the units and tens when presenting the results.

Resources

Linking cubes

Next step

Knowing what each digit in two-digit numbers represents and knowing that 0 is a legitimate place holder in the same way as the numbers 1–9.

0 as place holder

Learning outcome

To know what each digit in a two-digit number represents including 0 as a place holder (Y2)

Assumed knowledge and experience

The children should have had a great deal of practical work involving grouping at least nineteen objects and hopefully up to 30 or 40, into tens and units. They should also have experience of recording the results of the grouping in a clear and consistent way; for example, 3 tens 7 units means 37.

Mathematical importance

Understanding the value of place is essential to all number work. The children must have a deep understanding that the position of each digit matters greatly. Because children usually consider 0 to mean nothing, they may find it hard to accept that it is a vitally important component when working with numbers, and, like the wheel, which shares the same shape, one of the great inventions!

Activities

With the whole class together, write a number like 27 on the board. Ask the children how many tens are represented in the number. Ask them how many units. Remind any who are making mistakes or who seem unsure that 27 means 2 tens and 7 units. Explain that it is too awkward to always write 'tens' and 'units' so we simply miss out these words. Repeat with some different numbers. On the board, write a random collection of numbers from 10 to 100. Point to various numbers in turn and have the children write down the value of what is being pointed at. Individual whiteboards are very useful for this exercise as instant responses can be gained from the whole class. Watch and listen for accurate responses. If 35 is the number and the 3 is being pointed to, make sure the children write '30', 'thirty' or 'three lots of ten'.

Prepare up to nine 'ten sticks' and have nine units available. Pick up at random some sticks and units and place them on an OHP so that the images are cast on the screen. Have the children write down the

number that is represented. After a while, place two 'ten sticks' on the OHP and ask the children to write down the number they represent. Most children should understand that the number 20 is being represented and will write 20. Some may not and at this point it is important to stress that the 0 is very important and must be there. Ask the children if they would prefer £2 or £20! Stress the point again and repeat the work with other multiples of 10.

Use prepared activity sheets to begin formalising the work. Have activity sheets that contain questions such as: 24 = ? + 4; 46 = 40 + ?; 30 + 7 = ?

Make the work more real by using 10p and 1p coins. Have the children make up values such as 57p by using as few coins as possible. Ask the children questions like: 'How many 10ps would be the same as 60p?', 'I have three 10ps and eight 1ps. How much do I have?', 'How many 10ps will I need to make 87p? How many 1ps will I need?'

Points to watch

The failure to recognise the 0 as important must be addressed swiftly.

Resources

OHP; cubes; individual whiteboards; plastic coins (10p and 1p)

Next step

Know what each digit in a three-digit number represents (Y3).

Reinforcing activities

Learning outcome

To confidently talk about and use the language of place value with two-digit numbers (Y1 and Y2)

Assumed knowledge and experience

Children should be aware that numbers between 9 and 100 are composed of a digit that represents the tens value and another that represents the units. They should also know that 0 is a valid place holder.

Mathematical importance

Understanding place value is very important because it enables children to manipulate numbers at a later stage.

Activities

An abacus is a very good visual tool for showing place value and the way in which numbers grow. This activity is for small groups. Give each child an abacus and allow them to play with it for a few minutes. Now have them move the beads so that 0 is shown in each column. Ask them how they think we could show 5, for example. Reinforce the point that the beads must be placed in the correct column. Add on beads one at a time until 9 is reached. Now ask them to add one more. This may lead to discussion that 'the column is full' or 'there's no room'. Some children may realise that a bead has to be placed in the tens column. Explain to the children that we use the second column to represent tens numbers. Now have the children place two beads in the tens column and ask what number is being represented. If this is successful, begin to work with beads on the tens and units columns. Ask the more able children what they think the other columns may be for.

Once the activities above have been done, go on to more abstract form by giving the children a selection of activity sheets. Some activity sheets can contain a series of blank abacuses with the number to be represented below each one. The children must draw the beads in the correct positions. Other abacuses can be complete with beads and the children must write the number that is shown.

Set the children a homework task of collecting lots of a single item, for example, conkers, leaves, pencils, felt-tips or building bricks. Have each table make a display of their objects and make the table responsible for counting the numbers of each object and writing labels.

Human abacus! Use some PE hoops as 'beads' and arrange two children as the tens and units columns. Give out hoops to the rest of the class; colour coding might be useful if a selection is available. A child can call out a number and the other children have to take it in turns to put hoops over the 'columns'. The children acting as columns will need to put their arms out to stop the hoops falling on the floor. Encourage the children to call out if the correct number of hoops have been placed!

Points to watch

Displaying multiples of 10 in the units column.

Resources

Abacus (it is useful to have available a variety of abacus types so that children can appreciate that they do not all look the same); PE hoops

Next step

Place value with hundreds.

Ordering

Numbers are very often used to help make comparisons. This is often seen in such things as elections or end of Key Stage assessments! In making comparisons, ranking quantities and amounts by order of size is a very important skill. It is often useful in the real world. The language used at an adult level is very similar to that used by young children when beginning ordering work. Words and phrases such as 'more than', 'less than', 'greater', 'lesser', 'less', 'least', 'fewer', 'above', 'below', 'next to' and 'above' are very common. Very often, children have heard these words used before they come to school and have a fair general understanding of their meaning. As in so many other ways, the job of the teacher is to structure this informal learning and place it in the context of mathematics. With much ordering work, this leads on to the use of symbols, especially the = sign which shows parity, the > and < signs indicating the lesser or greater amount.

Knowing the numbers well enough to order them in various ways is also a prerequisite skill for gaining a good understanding of addition and subtraction. To know that one number is more than another implies that something has been done to the smaller number to change it into the larger one. What has been done and how?

The beginnings of teaching ordering with children need to be practical and visual. The informal knowledge they already have needs to be focussed. Just ordering children by height is an opportunity to use the correct language that will be useful in future work. When more formal lessons begin, objects should be used to illustrate that one group has more or less than another. Later the number line and number square are essential. All of this should lead most children to be able to write and speak using comparative language without the need for assistance from materials.

Comparing and ordering

Learning outcome

To understand and use the vocabulary of comparing and ordering numbers (Y1)

Assumed knowledge and experience

Children should have been given opportunities to compare quantities and amounts. These are likely to have included work with sand and water as well as numbers of objects during counting activities. They are likely to be familiar with words and phrases such as 'bigger', 'smaller', 'greater', 'fewer' and 'is the most/least'.

Mathematical importance

Comparing numbers and amounts is a fundamental mathematical skill which leads on to equality between numbers. The vocabulary introduced on this page is likely to come before the more formal 'more than/ less than' and is an important progression point. 'More than', 'less than' and 'between' are the subject of page 22.

Activities

Arrange for the children to have use of the school hall. They do not need to be changed for PE but bare feet are probably best. Place two PE mats on the floor, separated by some distance. Tell the children that when you clap your hands, they must move to one mat and stand on it. When this has been done, ask 'Which mat has the most children?', 'Which mat has the fewest children?'. Bring the class back and place a third mat on the floor. Repeat the exercise but this time have the children invent a statement which must use comparative language, for example, 'Our mat has the greatest number of children', 'Our mat has the least number', 'This mat has about the same number as that mat'.

Have available a non-fiction and a fiction text appropriate to Year 1. They may be books currently being used as part of the literacy work. Big books would be best. Before the lesson, ensure that the two books have a fairly obvious variance in the picture and word contents on at least some pages. The non-fiction text should clearly have more words per page and probably more illustrations overall.

Tell the children that they are going to be comparing the books for the number of pictures and words. Choose two children to hold up the books. Ask a child to give a page number and both books are

opened at that page. After a short discussion of the pages, tell the children you want them to use particular comparing words. Write these words on the board: high, higher, highest, low, lower, lowest. Begin discussing the pages, first by asking questions of the children such as 'Which page has the highest number of words?', 'Which page has a low number of words?', 'Does this page have a higher number of pictures than this page?'. It is likely that some debate will follow each question and this should be encouraged as long as the focus remains on the use of comparative language. Follow this up by the children making statements about the pages, for example, 'Emma's page has a high number of pictures but a low number of words'.

Make a space in the room and divide the class into groups so that each contains an obviously different number of children. Group sizes will vary according to the number in the class but something like two, four, eight and twelve are suggested. Each group must begin by making a statement about the other groups; for example, 'Sahib's group has a greater number than Pasha's'. Next, they must make a statement about their own group; for example, 'We have fewer children than Darius's group'.

Points to watch

No use of the focus vocabulary or misplaced use.

Resources

The school hall or playground if weather permits; PE mats; fiction and non-fiction texts

Next step

Move on to the use of formal language with 'more than', 'less than', 'between' and the use of the = sign to express equality.

Ordinal numbers

Learning outcome

To know the ordinal numbers to at least 20 (Y1)

To compare and order ordinal numbers to at least 100 (Y2)

Assumed knowledge and experience

The children should be aware of comparative language, such as 'greater', 'fewer', 'most', 'last', 'first', 'next to'. They are likely to know some of the earlier ordinals because of birthdays and be generally aware that all numbers can be expressed in an ordinal style by slightly changing the sound of the words.

Mathematical importance

Children need to know that ordinal numbers represent position. The idea of ordinal numbers representing position can be difficult for some children and so it is important that they have a firm grasp of the cardinal numbers before specific lessons on the ordinals.

Activities

The vocabulary of ordinal numbers to 20 is best done through constant 'drip feeding' as well as specific lessons. For example, when the children are lining up for assembly, ask them who is at a certain position, for example, fourth, eleventh, eighteenth. Each of the ordinals has enough of a clue in the sound of the word when spoken clearly by an adult to be fairly straightforward. Children must also have activities where they show understanding by saying the words themselves. Use a book such as Penny Dale's *Ten in a Bed* (Walker Books) which illustrates the famous rhyme with a little boy's cuddly toy animals. Have the children say which animal was first, seventh, tenth.

Have each child bring in a small toy – not too precious to the child or valuable! Arrange them in a straight line on the floor. Place a number card stating 5, 10, 15 and 20 against the appropriate toy. Go beyond 20 to 25 and 30 if needed. Ask the whole class questions like 'What is the seventh toy?', 'Who does the fifteenth toy belong to?' and 'Which toy is in the nineteenth position?'. Now have each child invent a question of their own to ask the rest of the class. Insist on use of the ordinals by each child. You may want to differentiate the questions so that the less able children use ordinals to 10, the main group to 20 and the most able children between 20 and 30.

Work on the ordinals to 100 can continue with the multiples of 10, for example, tenth, twentieth, thirtieth. Note that the children are only required to begin to read the ordinals at this stage and may be able to record the early ordinals.

Have Year 2 children listen carefully when some ordinals are said to them, for example, ninety-second. Use individual whiteboards and, after a few examples, have the children write down the cardinal number represented by the spoken ordinal, for example, ninety-second will be 92. As long as the children have a firm understanding of the sound of the ordinals to 9, they should have enough clues in the word sounds to be able to establish the corresponding cardinal number. Reverse the process and have the children write down a number of their own and then individually say the ordinal to the class or have others say it. You may want the whole class to chorus the answer as each number is shown. Make a display or class book of ordinals and have children bring examples, for example, 'My Gran's 80th birthday', 'My football team is seventeenth in the league', 'Our house is 44th in the street'. Advent is a good time of year to cover ordinals!

Points to watch

Children who have not grasped reading and saying numbers to 100.

Next step

Writing the ordinals in words and abbreviated forms.

Resources

Counting rhymes and stories; individual whiteboards

More than, less than, between

Learning outcome

To compare two familiar numbers, using 'more' or 'less' (Y1)

To compare two given two-digit numbers, say which is 'more' or 'less' and give a number 'between' (Y2)

Assumed knowledge and experience

The children should have a very good knowledge of the numbers to 100. They should have experience saying them, recognising the figures, understanding the order and of beginning to write them using words, as well as experience using comparative language such as 'highest', 'next to' and 'fewer'.

Mathematical importance

The ability to state which is more or less is an important life skill. At this stage, children may simply want to compare amounts of money but later they will need to be able to make more complicated comparisons such as prices based on cost per 100 g.

Activities

In Year 1, it is appropriate to begin with some simple matching work. Place seven objects in one set and five in another, then have the children remove simultaneously one object from each set. Which set has the most/least? After a few examples, formally introduce the phrases 'more than' and 'less than'. Now repeat the matching exercises but this time using phrases such as 'This set has more than/less than this one'.

During the course of the Year, give opportunities for use of 'more', 'less', 'most' and 'least' by asking questions, such as 'How many more on this table than that one?', 'Who has the most house points?', 'Which team has the least points?', 'Who had the most for lunch today?' and 'Did Darius score less or more than Emma?'.

With familiarity of the terminology, Year 2 children should undertake activities with larger numbers and in more formal settings. Prepare four sets of cards, each set with the numbers 0–9. Have two children stand to one side of the room with two more on the other side. Give each child a set of the cards. Ask the children to shuffle the cards. Now have the children

with the cards take the top card and display it. Two two-digit numbers will be formed. Ask questions using the more/less vocabulary. Select the next cards in the set and repeat. Discuss the situation if a 0 should be selected in the tens position.

Using a number line from 1 to 100, mark any two numbers. Explain that the children must give a number between the two selected numbers. Explain the meaning of 'between'/'in between', being sure to point out that the numbers themselves cannot be counted; for example, if 6 and 9 are selected, 6 and 9 cannot be 'between'. Ask questions relating to the selected numbers; for example, 'Give me a number between 50 and 60' and ask the children to write their answers on individual whiteboards or paper. This gives you the facility of seeing that each child has given an appropriate answer. Repeat, using 'more', 'less' and 'between' with as many numbers as time permits.

Ask the children to record some answers in words; for example, '73 is less than 81', '36 is more than 7', '19 lies between 12 and 27'.

Points to watch

Less able children struggling with 'more' and 'less' with the higher numbers.

Resources

Sets of 0–9 number cards; individual whiteboards; 1–100 number line

Next step

Use of < and > symbols.

The = sign and comparing

Learning outcome

To use the = sign to represent equality (Y1)

Assumed knowledge and experience

The children should have a good knowledge of the numbers to at least 20. They should have had opportunities to use comparative language such as 'more', 'less', 'higher', 'lower' and 'fewer'.

Mathematical importance

Until now, the children have only used general terms relating to comparisons; for example, 'more'. The use of the = symbol to represent equality now enables children to show when two quantities or amounts are the same. The use of the sign in addition and subtraction sums is an important step in formalising the written processes.

Activities

Warm up the children with some comparative language work with numbers up to 20. Remind them of symbols they have used for addition (+) and subtraction (–). Write on the board a simple number sentence such as '2 add 1 is the same as 3'. Have the children read it out and ask them if it is true. Write another sentence beneath the first one, again using the phrase 'is the same as'. Repeat once more. Now tell the children that it is really boring writing 'is the same as' every time and you know a symbol which means the same thing. Ask them if they know what it is. You may want to discuss their responses. Now place the = sign above the 'is the same as' part of the top number sentence. Explain that the = sign represents 'is the same as' and saves us lots of time. Ask two children to write the symbol on the board and have a few children describe what the sign looks like.

Individual whiteboards are best for the next activity; otherwise paper or books may be used. Have the children write a few simple addition number sentences of their own using the = sign. Inspect the answers for accuracy. Repeat a few times to ensure they are using the sign properly. Give some simple addition sums to the children but with the = sign missing, for example, 4 + 3 7 and 6 5 + 1. Be sure to vary the position of the total. Have the children place the = sign correctly. This is practice in writing the symbol itself.

The children now need to move on to using the = sign to show equality in the traditional way. Write a simple number sentence on the board, for example, 4 + 1. Ask the children what this sum equals. If children are unsure, revert to the phrase 'is the same as' but keep telling the children that 'equals' is the proper mathematical word. When children respond with the correct answer, write '5' on the board leaving a gap for the sign. Now have a child come to the board and place the sign in the correct position. Repeat this several times with different number sentences. Give the children plenty of practice on paper.

Continue in this vein with simple subtraction sentences and additions with more than two numbers for the more able children.

Prepare some digit sets of cards and cards showing +, – and = signs. Using the children to hold the cards, have them make number sentences using the digits and the symbols. Have the children say the sentences out loud each time to reinforce the correct language.

Points to watch

Poor writing of the = sign.

Resources

Number cards and cards showing +, – and = symbols

Next step

Ensuring throughout the year that the = sign is being written correctly and positioned properly within number sentences.

One more or less

Learning outcome

To say the number that is one more or less than any given number (to 20) (Y1)

Assumed knowledge and experience

The children should be familiar with the language of comparison. They should have experience of reading, saying and naming numbers to at least 20.

Mathematical importance

This work is an important step between knowing 'more than' and 'less than' and addition and subtraction. It is closely related to counting. Language to be introduced or revised includes 'before' and 'after'.

Activities

Use a 1–20 number line. With the whole class, have a child point to a low number, such as 5. Tell the children that we want to know the number that is one more than 5. Explain to the children that this is more precise than 'more than' which they used in previous lessons. Ask the children to think about the number that is one more than 5. Ask for suggestions. Through the suggestions, discuss the idea that 'one more than' means the same as 'the number after'. When the correct answer is given, tell the children explicitly that 'one more than' means the 'next number after'. Now give more opportunities to work with 'one more than' with numbers up to 20. After some verbal practice, ask the whole class to write down some responses on paper or their own whiteboards. Give a range of questions that go up to at least 20.

Repeat the activity using 'one less than' and explaining that this means 'the number before'. Do not be afraid to simply tell the children the meaning and then help deepen their understanding through examples as with 'one more than'.

To follow up the introductory lesson, prepare a blank number line that just shows marks to represent the numbers and write the number 8 in the correct position. Ask the children to tell you the numbers that are one more than/less than 8. Write the numbers on the line. Continue in the same way until the line is complete to 0 and 20.

Repeat the work, starting with a different number.

Stand ten children in a row and give out number cards to 10. Have the rest of the class answer questions such as 'Who is one more than Jared?', 'Who is one less than Sarah?', 'Is Annie one more or one less than Sandeep?'. Change the children and repeat the activity.

Now use prepared number lines from 1 to 20 but with single blank spaces at various points along the line. Give these out and have the children complete the lines by filling in the missing spaces. The more able children could have lines with more than single spaces, for example:

1 – – 4 – – – – 9 – 11 – – – – – 17 – – –

Put the objective into 'real life' problems. Ask questions such as 'How much is 1p more than 12p?', 'What is the date before 9 November?' and 'What is one day less than fourteen days?'.

Points to watch

Poor memory of number order when the numbers are not shown.

Resources

Individual whiteboards; 1–20 number line; blank number line with marks to represent 1–20

Next step

Working out the numbers that are ten or a hundred more or less than a given figure.

Ten or hundred more or less

Learning outcome

To say the number that is ten/hundred more or less than any given two-digit number (Y2)

Assumed knowledge and experience

The children should be very familiar with the numbers 1 to 100. They should be able to read and say the figures and some of the words. Familiarity with a range of more than/less than type situations is also important.

Mathematical importance

This work deepens the knowledge of numbers and how they relate to each other up to 100 and beyond when multiples of 100 are considered. It will become an element of addition and subtraction in mental and written forms.

Activities

Begin by counting on in tens using a number line. Initially count only the multiples of 10 but after a short while extend the activity by counting on in tens from any number. After a while, perform the same activity but using a 1–100 number square – the larger the better for the whole class part of the lesson. If individual whiteboards are being used, the metallic varieties have small magnetic number squares which may be used in the follow-up group work.

On the large board, colour the starting figure and then have the whole class count on in units up to 10 and then colour in that number. Repeat a few more times with the whole class counting on. Stop the children and ask if they can see a pattern developing. After discussion, ask them to predict what the next amount will be. Count on in units again and see if the predictions are correct. Repeat a few times and then do a similar activity but using different starting numbers.

Still using the large number square, point to numbers at random and ask the children to give the number that is ten more than. Repeat several times. Have some children give the initial number for a variation. After time spent on ten more than, tell the children that they will now examine ten less than. Repeat with similar activities and help the children to understand that this operation, subtraction, is the inverse of addition.

Give children a 1–100 number square and tell them that they are going to produce families of numbers. Have them colour in any two-digit number. Now give out a separate activity sheet that is labelled with ten more than/less than columns. Each child should write the starting number in the star at the top of the family, for example, 54, then complete the columns with 44, 34, 24, 14 and 4. Repeat with the children using different starting numbers. Some children will need the support of the number squares but many will not and after a while they should work without one.

Using a good supply of plastic 10p and 1p coins, have the children make amounts as they wish. They should record the amount in the normal format, for example, 36p. The less able children may use the coins to work out 10p more or less but the majority of the group should be able to calculate without support. Give some 'real life' problems such as 'Billy has 45p pocket money, Stacey has 10p more. How much does Stacey receive?'.

Use a blank number line marked with equally spaced units and begin the children counting in multiples of 100. Find out if they know what will follow 100. Complete the line and give practice with hundred more/less than questions.

Points to watch

The less able children miscounting when using the number line and square. Any children who fail to see the pattern when the number square is being used.

Resources

Large 1–100 number square; 1–100 number line; individual whiteboards; small magnetic 1–100 number squares; activity sheets as described

Next step

Adding one/ten/hundred up to 1000 (Y3)

Order whole numbers to 100

Learning outcome

To order whole numbers to at least 100, position on a number line and number square (Y2)

Assumed knowledge and experience

The children should have a good knowledge of reading and saying the numbers to 100. They should also have an understanding of comparative language such as 'more than' and 'less than'. They should have worked with number lines and number squares.

Mathematical importance

Ordering of numbers and amounts according to size is a very important skill, not just in mathematics, but across other curriculum areas such as ICT, geography and history. In mathematics, it has particular importance when handling data.

Activities

Prepare a set of cards that show some two-digit numbers, for example, 16, 25, 12, and 19. Shuffle the cards and have a group of children place them in order with the smallest on the left and the highest on the right. This is probably suitable for less able children who may need the support of a number line.

Repeat this with a wider range of numbers and some numbers that show reversals, for example, 74, 47, 92, 80 and 29.

Prepare a series of number lines where numbers have been misplaced. The children must spot the incorrect positioning and write the numbers in the proper order.

Make an opportunity for the children to order numbers across a tens boundary; for example, 49, 50 and 51.

Give the children random groups of numbers that need to be sorted into order. Be explicit about whether the lowest or the highest number should go first. Although the usual convention is to begin with the smallest number on the left, working the other way round is sometimes used and will help to reinforce the idea of order not being relevant to a particular starting point.

Have the children prepare some personal information, such as how much pocket money they receive, approximately how long they spend watching television, how many story books they have at home, the number of their house, and so on. Use this information and have the children order their personal information in relation to other groups. These groups can be changed to make even better use of the information. Begin with the children on one table, move on to the boys and girls separately, then within houses, then the whole class.

History timelines are a good opportunity for ordering although with young children the events may need to be vague, for example, the war, the Romans, or historically close, such as Christmas, birthdays, summer holidays. Use blank number lines and have some children give numbers from 1 to 100. Have all of the children mentally arrange the numbers in order. Ask one child to place a selected number on the line. Ask the rest of the class if it is in about the right place. Continue with the other numbers until the numbers have all been used. Repeat the activity.

Points to watch

Misunderstanding two-digit numbers that share the same digits, for example, 47 and 74.

Resources

Various types of number lines

Next step

Order to at least 1000.

Estimating

Estimation is a very useful life skill and helps adults out in all sorts of ways. In the supermarket, we can quickly round prices to the nearest pound and keep count as we go along. When decorating, we can decide on the tins of paint or rolls of wallpaper that may be needed. When organising parties, we can work out the number of cakes and packets of sausage rolls that might be needed. Such estimations actually involve approximation first. Estimation is not the same as approximation. Making approximations helps us to make an estimate. In the following activities, we will use approximation strategies to help make estimations.

It is important to tell children from the outset that an estimate is a sensible guess. The word 'sensible' cannot be over-emphasised. This is especially true with very young children who are unsure of numbers and will often go from 1, 2 and 3 to lots! A basic knowledge of the number structure is essential to this work.

An important part of approximation and estimation is developing simple strategies to help the process. Clearly, experience plays a large part in successful estimation. Very young children do not have much experience of estimation so need help. When working out a number of objects, young children might divide them into two groups that appear roughly equal. The smaller group size may help them to approximate and then, through doubling, the estimate can be reached.

At Key Stage 1, the required vocabulary is straightforward and consists mostly of 'to the nearest' and 'rounding'. Rounding to the nearest ten is usually simply taught as long as the children understand the structure of the number system to 100. Although estimation can be used to reinforce knowledge of the structure, it is best to focus on the rounding skill. When some confidence exists, the majority of the children can use numbers to 100 with some certainty.

Sensible guesses to 20/50, vocabulary

Learning outcome

To make sensible guesses up to twenty objects (Y1)

To use and begin to read the vocabulary of estimation and approximation to at least 50 objects (Y2)

Assumed knowledge and experience

The children should have a developing knowledge of the number shapes and names to at least 20.

They should also have some idea of the numbers representing the size or amount. This work needs to be done alongside counting on in ones.

Mathematical importance

Estimation gives children the ability to work things out roughly and then compare this with what should be a more accurate count.

Activities

Begin by having a very small number of objects, for example, two or three. Ask if the children can estimate – make a sensible guess – as to how many are there. Some will be able to count the actual number. Repeat with slightly more, for example, four or five, and ask for another estimation. Ask if this is more difficult. Now put out about ten objects and ask for an estimation. Try not to use the word 'guess'. Allow the children lots of opportunities to estimate with numbers up to 10, mainly so they can begin to hear the vocabulary being used.

Now start again with four objects but lay them out in a square pattern as if they were the dots on a dice. Repeat the estimating and then ask if it were any easier this time. Repeat with the numbers through to 10, laying them out in simple patterns. This is a simple strategy which children need to be taught as part of estimation and leads on to sampling in work such as statistical analysis. This activity is best done in small groups. Depending upon the ability of the group, place a random selection of objects on the table; small cubes or counters are suitable. The less able children may only have ten to fifteen, the main group up to 30 and the most able up to 50.

The activity is concerned with developing sensible guesswork as much as it is about achieving correct answers. Ask the children in the groups to look at the

objects and without saying anything, make an estimate of the number. After a short while, have them write their estimate down on paper or a whiteboard. Go around and ask for estimations, using the vocabulary: 'Jack, what is your estimate?', 'Reba, how many have you estimated?', 'Moira, what is your estimation?' Discuss the result. You will only be looking for children who are a long way out; those who are correct or who have come close should be congratulated.

If children have not come close, they must be told to improve their estimation by making a more sensible guess. Repeat the activity but this time allow the children a few minutes on their own to rearrange the objects and give them some sort of order. It may be that the children will separate them into small groups, count one group and then calculate from there. Although this is likely to be a difficult task for young children, they should be encouraged to look for strategies to help estimations.

Prepare activity sheets with various numbers of dots on them, the more different activity sheets the better. Differentiate the sheets. Make spaces for five children to write their estimates on each sheet. Pass the activity sheets around and, after a suitable amount of time, discuss the estimates with each group.

Points to watch

Hopelessly inaccurate estimates. Failure to produce simple strategies.

Resources

Small cubes and counters; selection of objects; random dot activity sheets

Next step

Rounding to nearest ten.

Rounding to nearest ten

Learning outcome

To round numbers less than 100 to the nearest ten (Y2)

Assumed knowledge and experience

The children should have a good knowledge of number names to 100 and be able to use comparative language such as 'more than' and 'less than'.

Mathematical importance

Rounding is a useful tool in many 'real life' situations such as working out monthly bills! It is also a useful tool when checking results of complicated calculations.

Activities

Explain to the children that rounding is a useful way of making life a bit easier and they are going to learn about rounding numbers to the nearest ten. Demonstrations should be visual to begin with. Draw a number line from 10 to 20. Have the children say the numbers between 10 and 20 and place them on the line. Now point to 19 and ask the children if they think it is nearer ('nearest') to 10 or 20 on the line. Most will recognise 20 as nearer and therefore 'nearest'.

Repeat this a number of times mainly emphasising the word 'nearest'. Do not use 15 as an example for now. Tell the children that finding the nearest ten is called 'rounding'. Introduce the term with 'We are going to be rounding numbers to the nearest ten'. Now use a number line from 30 to 40 and repeat the activity. Do not include 35.

Introduce numbers ending in 5 as a special case. Some children may have already noticed that it has not been included so far. Ask the children what they think will happen with 35 or 25 or 15. They will probably respond with 'it's halfway'. Tell them that mathematicians all over the world have agreed that numbers ending in 5 are always rounded up to the nearest ten. Ask a few simple questions to reinforce the point.

This next activity could take place in the hall. Give some children cards with the multiples of 10 in large print on them. Have these children position themselves around the hall. Call out various 'random' numbers and have the children run to the child who is holding the nearest ten card.

Repeat similar tasks using plastic coins and having the children taking amounts to the nearest 10p. Ask questions such as 'Sven has 17p. How much is that to the nearest 10p?', 'Angie needs 74p for a comic. Her father only has 10ps. How many will he need to give her?', 'Ulrika has fifteen house points. What is that to the nearest ten?'.

Using the plastic coins, have one child make up an amount; their colleague must round that to the nearest 10p.

Points to watch

Watch especially for the children who forget that 5 is always rounded up.

Resources

Number lines 10–20 and 30–40

Next step

Rounding to the nearest hundred.

Fractions

Most children come to school with a general awareness of fractions, especially halves and quarters, and have heard the words used as part of normal speech and interaction. Children are likely to understand halves and quarters in a general way that is not necessarily very mathematical. Some children may, however, have a very precise understanding, especially if they have a sibling with whom they have to share. Parents will often tell their children to share fairly. It is the idea of fair shares which can be translated into a mathematical definition of halves and quarters.

Fractions lead the way to division. Through the process of finding one-half or one-quarter, we are actually taking one whole number or amount and dividing it by two or four. Younger children are more likely to use the word 'sharing' than dividing but many are capable of understanding the concept of division.

It is most important that early work with fractions takes place with as many media as possible. These should include at least these three elements: 3-D work with folding and cutting paper; dividing groups of objects into smaller sets; questioning using 'real' situations, for example, 'How much is half of 20p?'.

The equivalence of fractions is important and whereas the idea of halves and quarters are usually picked up without too much trouble, equivalence can prove an early stumbling block. Many opportunities of showing equivalence with 3-D materials, probably paper, should be sought and the subject returned to as often as necessary for the less able children.

Encourage constant articulation of the vocabulary of fractions: whole, half, halves, halving, quarter, quarters, quartering, sharing, dividing.

Half and quarter

Learning outcome

To begin to recognise and find one-half and one-quarter of shapes and small numbers of objects (Y2)

Assumed knowledge and experience

Children will have heard simple fractions such as one-half and one-quarter talked about by parents, carers, older brothers and sisters and probably on television. Most children understand the general meaning of half and halves before they come to school although they may not know the mathematical idea of two equal shares.

Mathematical importance

Fractions are a mathematical way of talking about and using parts of whole numbers and amounts. They are a step on the way to learning about decimals and percentages.

Activities

Ideally this activity should start with a cake, some sweets or some fruit which can be shared among the children; they will pay more attention than if counters are used! Have the children sit in their own places and tell them that you are going to split them into two equal groups. One at a time, tell each child to take a place on either your right or left side. Once this has been done, have the children count out loud how many are in each group. If there is an odd number, join the group with the smaller number. Tell the children that they have now been divided into two equal groups and that we call each group one-half. Write 'one-half' on the board and tell them that we write this as ½. Explain that this symbol means the one on top is shared between the two on the bottom.

Now place a cake before them and tell them that you are going to share it equally between the two groups. Emphasise the equal shares. Pretend to cut off one piece which is obviously not one-half and ask if this is right. After some teasing, agree with the two groups where cutting into equal parts would be correct. Cut the cake and explain that it has been cut into two equal parts and that each part is called one-half.

Give out prepared activity sheets which contain line drawings of simple shapes. Tell the children that they must cut out the shapes, then halve their appearance by folding the cut-out. Note that if time permits, it would be best to cut out the shapes beforehand, as cutting out is not the focus of this lesson! Let the children cut out the shapes and try folding them until the new shape appears to be half the original shape. If the paper has been folded in half, no 'bits' should show around the edges. Once this has been done, have the children cut down the fold line and create two halves of each shape. Write 'one-half' and 'two halves' on the board and point out the difference with the plural.

Give each table a set of up to twenty objects. This work should be differentiated by number of objects. Have two children on each table take one away from the objects, one at a time. This will reinforce the idea of equal shares. When all of the objects have been removed, have the children count how many are in each collection. Tell the children to write a number sentence such as 'We have found out that 5 is half of 10'. Some children will probably need help in scribing this. Move the collections around to different tables and repeat the activity.

Repeat the activity with one-quarter but constantly reinforce the idea that one-quarter means sharing in four equal quarters. Explain that the ¼ symbol means one group shared equally between four.

Points to watch

Children who just separate the groups into two, irrespective of whether they are equal amounts.

Resources

Plenty of groups of different objects – counters and cubes would do

Next step

Recognising the equivalence between simple fractions.

Equivalence

Learning outcome

To begin to recognise that two halves or four quarters make one whole and that two-quarters and one-half are equivalent (Y2)

Assumed knowledge and experience

The children should have experience working with simple shapes that may be halved or quartered through folding. They should have experience with folding to check that both parts are equal and cutting to create halves. They should understand through sharing between two/four that a half/quarter means creating two/four equal amounts or parts.

Mathematical importance

As with the English language, mathematics has different ways of saying the same thing. Likewise with fractions; two fractions although having different appearances can be equivalent.

Activities

The class can work in small groups. Give each group two large sheets of sugar paper. Remind the children of the work they have already carried out with fractions. Especially remind them that half and quarter means sharing in equal parts. Have the children divide one sheet into halves by folding, checking that the parts are the same, then cutting it out. The children should label each part clearly with 'half' and '½'. Now ask the children to cut the other sheet into quarters and label them as 'quarter' and '¼'. Ask the children to investigate if any combination of the quarter parts is the same as one-half. This is likely to only take a few minutes. Have each group hold up their two quarters and the equivalent one half. Make it explicit that it works for all the tables.

Ask the children to tell you a sentence which sums up what they have found out. They should articulate something like 'Two-quarters are the same as one-half'. Please note that this work is based on the probability that the children will halve and quarter the paper on vertical and horizontal lines. It is possible that children will halve and quarter in other ways, especially the diagonals. Should this happen, allow time for discussion and congratulate the children for finding different ways but base the focus of the lesson on the normal method.

Give out sets of objects to each table. Each set should be a multiple of 4. The number of objects can be differentiated to suit ability groups. Have the children sort the group into two halves. One child should act as a scribe and write a sentence to say how many are in half the set; for example, 'One-half of 12 is 6'. Now recombine the set and ask the children to quarter it. The scribe then writes something like 'One-quarter of 12 is 3'. Now ask the children to put two-quarter sets together and write a third sentence such as 'Two-quarters are 6'. At this point, ask if another fraction was also 6. After discussion and ensuring everyone has the same result, write on the board that two-quarters are the same as one-half. The word 'equivalent' may be used with the whole group and some should remember it.

Have each child think of one object that can be halved and one that can be quartered. Allow each child to contribute to a class 'Halves and Quarters' display through suggestion, drawing or bringing actual objects. Use a 0–10 number line that has large gaps between each number. Ask the children where the halves may go. Use the line and have children come to show where numbers like 4½ might be. Draw a straight line and ask a child to mark in black where halfway is. Have another child mark in red where the quarter marks might go. Does the red two-quarters mark match the black half mark?

Points to watch

Confusion arising through different ways of halving and quartering the sugar paper.

Resources

Sugar paper; sets of objects – counters or cubes would do; 0–10 number line

Next step

Working with tenths which leads to decimals.

Addition and subtraction

Mathematics is a gradual building process where more and more complex situations and structures are added to the basic ideas over a period of years. All number work in school begins with the children being able to read, write, say and understand the number system to ever increasing levels. Most children reach a good understanding of numbers and amounts to 100 in Key Stage 1 and many are able to deal with numbers up to 1000.

Once familiarity with the number system starts, various ways of manipulating the numbers begin to be introduced. Infants usually encounter their first experiences of manipulating numbers and amounts with addition and subtraction. Most children find addition an easier process than subtraction for one particular reason. Whereas addition can be done in any order, subtraction has to be done in a specific order. Addition also tends to have fewer words to represent it (for example, 'plus', 'together', 'total') than subtraction which has 'minus', 'subtract', 'reduce', 'difference', 'take away'. It is no wonder that the subtraction process can easily confuse children.

Addition is introduced in the National Numeracy Strategy (NNS) through simple counting on in ones, probably using a number line. At this early stage, the term 'add' or 'addition' may not even be mentioned but rather, 'counting on' or 'counting back' will be used. The early language is likely to be along the lines of 'what number is one more than?' or 'what number is next to?'. Later on, children will come to see addition as a way of combining sets of numbers, amounts or objects. They will discover that addition means a growth in a number when it takes on board another number or set of numbers.

An important point for young children to realise is that the order of addition does not matter to the result. It will be the same whichever way round the numbers go. Children should also be told that although the order does not matter to the result, generally speaking, it is good to get into the habit of placing the largest number first. It is worth pointing out that the NNS encourages the use of counting on techniques, mental addition and recording of mental addition in horizontal form at Key Stage 1. The belief is that the usual vertical algorithm does not encourage understanding and is only learning a technique.

Subtraction must be handled with extreme care. Every step must be broken down into small chunks and imparted with sensitivity. Mistakes and misunderstandings must be picked up immediately and dealt with. A great strength with subtraction is that it can be explained and taught in a number of ways. Unfortunately, this is also its weakness as some children, particularly the less able, can easily become confused by the plethora of techniques and ways of wording problems involving subtraction. Subtraction can even be done by counting on from the lower number!

All addition and subtraction work should start with actual objects. Children need to be able to see what is happening, the effect of the operations. This can then move on to using smaller objects, like counters and cubes, and proper recordings of calculations may begin. Some children will no longer need visual and tactile assistance after a while and can move into writing number sentences with confidence. The final step in Key Stage 1 is to have the ability to answer written and oral questions correctly. At all times, children should be encouraged to explain their thinking, their techniques and their strategies and to write down their methods.

Understanding addition

Learning outcome

To understand the process of addition and some of the associated vocabulary (Y1)

Assumed knowledge and experience

The children should have knowledge of the number system to 20 including reading, writing and saying the number names. They should also have experience with counting on and back in ones. They should have had some opportunities to use the = sign.

Mathematical importance

The children have had a small amount of experience with manipulating one set of numbers by counting on and back. Addition goes beyond this and allows children to work with two sets when combining them. Note that the NNS does not require formal recording using + and = signs at this stage and that the majority of early addition work is intended to be done mentally. Using 3-D aids is extremely important at this level.

Activities

As far as possible, after the initial activity, children should work in small groups and be supported by an LSA or other adult. Very sound understanding of the addition process is imperative. The whole group should sit in a circle. Place two biscuits on a plate in the centre of the circle. Motivate the children with 'Who likes chocolate biscuits?' type questions. Ask if it would be better to have more biscuits. The likely answer is 'yes' so take one biscuit from the packet and say that 'I am going to add one more. How many biscuits are there now?' With the answer three, tell the children that you have added one more and now there are three. Write on the board 'add' and 'added'. Now ask 'Shall we add some more?' and continue the process adding one at a time. After a few more additions, clear the plate leaving just one biscuit and add two biscuits, then one and begin to suggest that we can add any amount to any amount. Initially, it is acceptable to say 'Two and one make three' rather than use 'add' or 'equals' but the correct language should be used as soon as possible.

Give each group a card showing the word 'add' and another showing the = sign. Copy page 96 Shapes for counting from *Blueprints Maths Key Stage 1: Pupil Resource Book* and give it out to each group along

with scissors. Tell the children they will make their own adding sums and they must cut out some pictures and 'display' their own adding sums. The word 'addition' might be used with the main group and the more able children. Give the children time to cut out the symbols and experiment with making addition sums. Please note that ideally the shapes should already be cut, as this is not supposed to be a cutting exercise! Allow time for free making of sums and visit all the groups, encouraging correct use of language. Have some groups present their work to the rest of the class.

With the whole class, place two small sets of objects in the circle of children. Tell the children that the two groups or sets are going to be put together to find out the total. Explain that the total means the numbers in each group added together. Use a large + sign and put it between the groups or sets. Have the children move objects from one group to the other and explain as they go, for example, 'We started with three, we added one and now we have four'.

Once 'add', 'adding', 'addition', 'total', 'equals' are secure, reinforce with 'plus' and 'combine'.

Points to watch

Poor use of addition language. Low-level knowledge of number names.

Resources

Packet of chocolate biscuits; sets of objects; activity sheets

Next step

Use of the + sign and addition to 20 with mental strategies by bridging through 10.

Addition in any order/Using the + sign

Learning outcome

To begin to recognise that addition can be done in any order (Y1)

To begin to use the + sign when recording mental calculations (Y1)

Assumed knowledge and experience

The children should have experience working with combining two sets of objects. They should also have a good knowledge of number names to at least 20. They should also understand that a symbol can be used to replace a word or concept, for example, the = sign.

Mathematical importance

Understanding that addition can be done in any order is very helpful when undertaking calculations as it enables the opportunity to decide which numbers might form bonds to make the whole sum easier, for example, numbers which add to 10. It also enables checking the answer by adding in a different order. As with the = sign, the + sign is a useful shorthand which saves time. In all early recording work, you should use the traditional style of writing and reading the sum from left to right. Although children must come to understand that right to left is equally appropriate, it may confuse them at this important early stage.

Activities

Place two sets of interesting objects on the floor with the children sitting in a circle around the outside. Tell the children they are going to add the two sets together by moving objects from one group to the other. On completion, write the sum on the board using 'add' and the = sign. Put the objects back in their original sets and repeat but this time reversing the number of objects. Make sure the children understand that, for example, 3 + 4 gives the same total as 4 + 3. Repeat often and discuss. Make sure the children clearly see that reversing the numbers makes no difference to the total.

Write an addition sum using figures and the = sign but including 'add' rather than the + sign. Ask what the = sign means and then write 'equals' on the board. Explain that we use the sign because it saves us time and that people all over the world understand the sign whatever language they speak. Now tell them that we have a special sign for add and ask if anyone knows what it is. After a short while, draw the + sign and tell them it means add.

Break the class into small groups and give out cubes or counters. Also give to each group a card showing large + and = signs. Now have each group make up number sentences using the cubes or counters and

the signs. Each child should record a few example sums using numerals and signs. Check that they use the symbols correctly and that the totals are correct.

Stand three children in one group and two in another. Tell the children to write in books or on whiteboards 3 + 2 =. Have the children call out as first one child then the other moves from the smaller group to the larger. Complete the number sentence by writing 5. Now have the children write 2 + 3 =. Move the three children to the two and have the answer written again. Choose five different children and separate into a four and one. Repeat the exercise.

Give the children some prepared addition sums, for example, 6 + 2 = 8, and ask them to write the sum in a different way. Give each group ten counters. Have each child write down one way of adding two numbers to give the total of 10, for example, 7 + 3. Now ask each child to reverse the two smaller amounts and check using the counters that their answer is still true. Have them work out as many number combinations as they can to reach 10.

Ask children questions using as many different ways of saying 'add' as possible. Have a few of the questions and answers recorded using the correct symbols.

Points to watch

Failure to appreciate the reversal concept because of concentration on the correct addition. Failing to recognise the sums in symbolic form.

Resources

Cubes and counters; individual whiteboards

Next step

Adding more than two sets.

Number sentences

Learning outcome

To add in number sentences (Y1)

Assumed knowledge and experience

The children should have knowledge of numbers to at least 20. They will have growing experience with the vocabulary of addition. They should be able to recognise the + and = signs.

Mathematical importance

It is important for children to know that a number sentence contains information about the numbers or amounts involved in the problem and the remainder gives clues about the operation that needs to be performed.

Activities

Give a series of questions in number sentence form that use different words and phrases to represent the addition process. These may be given individually, in groups or to the whole class. Expect the children to concentrate hard and sort out the data from the operational requirements. The strategy of examining a question for clues as to the operation is very important and the children will benefit greatly from lots of practice. Begin with simple oral problems with low numbers; for example: add 3 and 5; what is 4 add 2; add 6 to 5; 8 add 2; what do 2 and 5 make; what do 7 and 1 equal; what is 6 plus 3; 5 plus 7 is; 2 plus 9 equals; what is the sum of 6 and 4; total 9 and 3; what is the total of 8 and 4; add 3 and 2 together; what is the total when 5 and 3 are added; find the sum of 4 and 4; put together 6 and 4; how many are 4 and 6; combine 4 with 6.

For the next activity, begin to put the addition problem into more complex form that will make the child ask 'What do I have to do?'. Children with a tenuous hold on the understanding of addition will flounder as the amount of information becomes too much to interpret. Return those children to oral work using objects if necessary. All of the following problems may be answered mentally or by use of apparatus for the less able children.

I add seven bricks to five bricks. How many bricks do I have altogether?

Darius has 6p. Emma has 8p. How much do they have in total?

What amount is equal to the total of 6 and 6?

How many children go on the trip if six go by coach and eight by car?

A useful activity for all the children irrespective of ability is to just have them write the number sentence in symbolic form for each of these problems; for example, if they are given 'Add 3 and 2 together' they would write something like 3 + 2, 2 + 3, 3 add 2, or 2 plus 3. The important thing to look for is recognition of the calculation that has to be gone through. Many children's mathematics fail to develop because although they can confidently work out a formal sum 7 + 3 =, they cannot decipher a 'real' question involving a process.

Points to watch

Difficulty in establishing what needs to be done.

Resources

Individual whiteboards might be useful; objects for the less able children

Next step

Addition with larger numbers up to a total of 100.

Symbols for unknown numbers

Learning outcome

To recognise the use of symbols to stand for unknown numbers (Y1)

Assumed knowledge and experience

The children should be familiar with numbers to at least 20 and have experience of the use of the + and = signs in addition to 20. They should have mental recall of addition facts to 5. They should know simple methods of recording mental processes.

Mathematical importance

This work leads into problem solving without using words. The idea of finding an unknown also presents a new challenge that can be met through mathematical method. A symbol representing an unknown quantity also suggests future work in algebra.

Activities

Tell the whole class that they are going to help solve a mystery. Write $5 + 2 = ?$ on the board. Ask the children what the '?' means, what it stands in place of. Some will give the actual answer but others might state that it stands for the mysterious missing number. Tell the children that the question mark stands for a mystery number that has to be found! Ask how the puzzle can be solved. Expect answers that use good mathematical vocabulary, for example, 'The question mark replaces the total of 5 and 2 which is 7'. Write five more puzzles on the board, all in the same format. Ask the children to solve just one problem but not to put up their hands. Begin with the top puzzle and ask for answers. Have some of the children explain verbally how they came to their answer. Make sure the correct answer comes forth with a good explanation. Move on to the next puzzle and repeat the exercise.

Follow up the activity with some practice in written form but using a variety of symbols in the answer position; ☐ is very common.

Give a 1–20 number line to each group. Give out prepared question sheets differentiated according to ability. The sheets should contain sums along the line of $12 + 6 = $ ☐.

Use plastic coins and make some available on each table. Ask the children to make up their own number sentences but not to put in an answer but just invent a mystery symbol to represent the answer. Make sure the 'p' symbol is used correctly. Encourage the more able children to place the mystery symbol on the left of the sum as well as on the right. Have the children pass their sums around to others on the table for solving.

Repeat the exercise with the children inventing a mystery sound to represent the symbol for an unknown number. Use tape recorders and have some children record their questions. The rest of the class can listen and then try to answer.

It is possible to have the symbol as part of the sum rather than representing the answer, for example, $6 + $ ☐ $ = 10$. Care needs to be taken with this format because subtraction could be used ($10 - 6 = 4$) but it will probably not have been fully taught or understood at this point. However, counting on from 6 to 10 using a number line is possible and legitimate at this stage and that is the method that the able and the more able children should be shown.

Most of the above exercises may be done orally and it will be more fun if you use an interesting noise-maker like a whistle or hooter to represent the unknown number.

Points to watch

Confusion of process when the unknown number is placed within the sum.

Resources

Coins; 1–20 number lines; tape recorder and cassette

Next step

Rapid recall addition with symbols to 10. Addition with counters, coins and number lines to 100.

Adding two or more numbers

Learning outcome

To recognise that more than two numbers can be added together (Y1 and Y2)

Assumed knowledge and experience

The children should have had experience adding two single digits together orally and recording the calculation using the + and = signs. They should have an understanding that addition involves combining one set of numbers or objects with another. They should know that the order in which numbers are added makes no difference to the total.

Mathematical importance

This work has significance in 'real life' problems where such things as lists are often totalled.

Activities

Place three PE hoops on the floor and have the children sit around them in a circle. Ask the children if they think it is possible to add more than two numbers or amounts together. After discussion, place one book in one hoop, two books in the second and three in the third. Have a child stand inside the first hoop and hold up the book. Now have another child lift up the second hoop with the two books, place the hoop over the head of the standing child and hand them the books. Repeat this with the third hoop so that the standing child now has three hoops and six books. Tell the children that they have now combined three sets of books (represented by the three hoops). Ask how many books are being held. Formalise this by writing the problem out as follows: $1 + 2 + 3 = 6$.

Repeat this exercise using different numbers of books and hoops. Make sure that the sum is written down each time so that the children become used to seeing a series of numbers with addition signs between them.

Ask the children to write a number between 3 and 20 on a piece of paper or on their whiteboards. Let them show their chosen number to the rest of the class. Tell them that you are going to write some addition sums on the board and if they think the answer matches the number they have written they may stand up. Write the first and second numbers slowly

and tease them a bit – will the total be their number! On writing the third number, see if anyone has the correct answer. At this point, either stop and see who was correct or write a fourth number. Now have each child write a few different sums that give the total they wrote. If they have a written a low number, just put a one in front of it!

Write the numbers 1, 2, 3, 4 and 5 on the board (1–20 for more able children). Ask the children to choose any three of the numbers and add them. This may be done mentally or by recording in the normal horizontal format. Less able children may use counters. Now have them use a different set of three numbers. Repeat the exercise. Ask them to total all of the numbers.

Using plastic 10p, 5p, 2p and 1p coins, have one child close their eyes and take a few coins at random. A few other children can do the same. Each child then writes down their own amount, the amounts of the their friends and the total.

Ask the more able children to give the total in a series of numbers, for example, 1–5, 3–8, 1–10. Make sure that the children have opportunities to add numbers that are not in order by size, for example, the total of 6, 17 and 8.

Points to watch

Missing the + sign when recording sums. Incorrect addition with larger groups.

Resources

PE hoops; individual whiteboards; plastic coins

Next step

Formal recording of addition sums which have been worked out mentally.

Adding three two-digit numbers

Learning outcome

To add three two-digit numbers with the help of apparatus (Y2)

Assumed knowledge and experience

The children should understand that more than two numbers may be added together. They should realise that the order of adding does not matter. They should be familiar with the numbers to 100, as well as with reading, writing and saying them. They should realise that a symbol can represent an unknown number.

Mathematical importance

This work consolidates the theory, process and practice of addition. It also involves a deepening understanding of place value to 100.

Activities

Prepare shopping lists for the children (see Activity sheet 34). These should contain three items and their prices. It would be best to differentiate the amounts so that the less able children have smaller amounts, possibly with some multiples of 10p. The main group could have a wider variety of amounts, possibly involving multiples of 5p or additions that do not cross the 10 boundary. The more able children could have larger amounts as long as the total does not exceed £1.00. Give out plastic coins and allow the children to create each of the three amounts separately and then give a total by combining the sets.

Use a 1–100 number line that is labelled at each five or ten but marked at each unit. Ask a child to tell you their birthday, use the day part as the first number. Repeat with two more children. It will not matter if the birthdays are before the tenth as the process will still be the same. These are the numbers to be added. Write the number sentence on the board and put a question mark after the equals sign. Mark the position of the first number on the number line. Count on with the second number and then the third. The children may want to give strategies to enable quicker counting on, for example, if 27 is added, it might be suggested that ten is added, then another ten, then the seven. This should be encouraged but not allowed to detract from the main focus. Give out a class list that shows the birthdays. Have the

children make up some of their own sums using information about their friends and find totals using a number line. Number squares may also be used for this although the visual impact is not so strong.

Write six two-digit numbers on the board. Have the children select three of the numbers and write them as a number sentence. Ask the children how they would try to find the total. After some discussion, work out the answer and write it on the board. Comment that the number 'seems very big' or 'doesn't seem very large', then ask them to try and think of three of the numbers that may give a larger/smaller total. Try out one of the suggestions and work it out using a number line. Challenge the children to use the six numbers to produce the biggest or smallest total they can.

Write a sum similar to the following on the whiteboard, $17 + 25 + ? = 58$.

Talk with the children about strategies they might use to find the mystery number. Tell the children that finding the total of the first two, then counting on to the 58 would be a reasonable strategy. Let them try it. Now give out a series of such sums and let them work them out. The more able children might cope with having numbers other than the last one missing but do not do this with the less able children as it will likely lead to confusion.

Points to watch

Miscounting when counting on with the number line.

Resources

Number lines 1–100; number squares; plastic coins

Next step

Adding a series of numbers so that the total is beyond 100.

Understanding subtraction

Learning outcome

To understand the operation of subtraction (Y1)

Assumed knowledge and experience

The children should have a knowledge of the numbers to at least 20. They should also know that a sign can stand in the place of a word, especially the = sign.

Mathematical importance

Subtraction is a life skill that is used by most people on a daily basis. Great care needs to be taken with teaching subtraction because there are different ways of thinking of it as a process and different strategies for working the computation. Subtraction may be thought of as working out the difference between two sets; it may also be considered as finding out by how much one set is less than another. Subtraction calculations may also be successfully worked out by adding on! Children can become easily confused so care is needed.

Activities

The children should sit on the floor in a circle. Place five sweets in a hoop on the floor. Tell the children that you are going to take one sweet away. Ask the children which one you should choose! Remove one sweet and ask the children how many are left in the hoop. Tell the children that you are feeling really greedy and want another sweet; say 'I am going to take another one'. Already, two forms of 'take' have been used. Ask if a child wants a sweet; 'Sata, would you like to take one?'. After each sweet is removed, have the children tell you the number left. When no sweets are left, put the five back in the hoop.

Tell the children they are going to talk about a long word called subtraction. Write 'subtraction' on the board. Ask the children how many sweets are in the hoops. Write '5' on the board. Now explain that there are many ways of saying subtract but for now they are going to think about taking away. Write 'take away' after the five. Ask the children how many you took away the first time and then write '1'. Then write the equal sign that they should be familiar with because of earlier work on addition. Take a sweet from the hoop and say 'five take away one is?'. Write '4' on the board to complete the number sentence. Repeat this until all the sweets have been removed.

Ask ten children to stand up. Tell a member of the class to take away one of the children and return them to their seat. Ask them how many are left. Have a different child take away another child. Ask how many are left now. Continue with this until none is left. With all the children sitting down, write the sums on the board, for example, 10 take away 1 is 9. Somewhere towards the end of the sequence, ask a child to 'remove' someone. Ask the class if they noticed what word you had used. Discuss the idea that sometimes we don't actually use the words 'take away' but words that mean the same thing. Do not labour the point for now.

Explain to the children using the examples on the board that, with subtraction, we have the larger number on the left. Although this is not always the case, working with negative numbers is very likely to confuse children at this stage.

Produce some cards which show 'take away' and =. Give out counters or cubes. Ask the children to invent their own small sums being sure to have the larger number on the left of the number sentence. The children can select a group of counters then place the 'take away' sign, then a second group of counters and finally the = sign. Another child can then work out the sum and the roles can be reversed.

Points to watch

Children failing to see that the result of subtracting is a reduction in group size.

Resources

Sweets; hoops; 'take away' and = cards; counters and cubes

Next step

Wider use of subtraction vocabulary.

Vocabulary of subtraction

Learning outcome

To understand a wider range of subtraction vocabulary

Assumed knowledge and experience

The children should know the number names to at least 20 and the correct use of the + sign. They should realise that mental processes may be written in a mathematical form. They should have some experience with the phrase 'take away' and its derivatives.

Mathematical importance

The phrasing of problems that result in a subtraction calculation are numerous. Children must know some of the most widely used words and phrases so that they understand the subtraction operation is involved. Great care must be paid in teaching this wider vocabulary as confusion about subtraction often sets in at this point.

Activities

Remind the children about using the expression 'take away' and work through a few simple examples with objects and by writing number sentences on the board.

With the children sitting in a circle, place five objects in a hoop on the left and two in another on the right. Ask the children if they can look at the objects and tell the difference in the numbers. Some uncertainty will show so ask them if they can tell you what 'the difference' between two numbers means. Write 'the difference between' on the board. After some discussion, tell the children that they are going to find the difference between the two sets of objects by taking one object from each set in turn. Place one child by each hoop. Have each child remove one object. Have the children remove another object from each set. This will result in one empty set. When this happens, have the children count how many objects remain in the left-hand set. Now write on the board '5 and 2 is 3'. This will complete the sentence which will read 'the difference between 5 and 2 is 3'.

Beneath this sentence write the number sentence '5 take away 2 = 3' and tell the children that finding the difference is very much like taking away; they are both forms of subtraction. Repeat the same exercise using a variety of objects.

Have the children work in pairs using cubes or counters. One child should make two small sets of objects and ask the other child to 'find the difference between them'. Insist on the children using exactly the right vocabulary. The other child can then either look and count the numbers in each set and work out the answer mentally, or remove one object from each set until one set is empty. The child must respond with 'The difference between the sets is' and finish the sentence with the correct answer. Swap the roles of the children. Repeat this exercise several times.

Draw eight blobs on the left of the board and two on the right. Ask the children how many more blobs are on the left than on the right. After allowing them time to think, ask for some answers and ask a few children who give correct answers to explain their methods. At least a couple of methods are likely. Tell the children that finding 'how many more' is yet another way of asking for a subtraction calculation to be carried out. Repeat this exercise with more examples.

Points to watch

Confusion between the terms now being used.

Resources

Sets of interesting objects; cubes and counters; hoops

Next step

Using the − sign and recording mental calculations using symbols.

The – sign; symbols for unknown numbers

Learning outcome

To begin to use the – sign when recording mental calculations (Y1)

To recognise the use of symbols standing for unknown numbers in number sentences (Y1)

Assumed knowledge and experience

The children should be familiar with the number names to at least 20. They should have experience with using the + sign and realise that symbols such as ? and ☐ may be used to represent unknown numbers. They should be able to do mental addition and transfer mental calculations to simple written formats.

Mathematical importance

The – sign is an important part of the mathematics vocabulary which will be used extensively from now on.

Activities

Remind the class of the way in which they have been setting out subtraction sums so far, for example, 7 take away 4 = 3. Tell the children that, just as we use the + sign as a simple way of representing addition, we have a special sign which indicates the operation of subtraction. Draw a – sign on the board and tell the children that we usually call this the minus sign and it means to take the smaller number from the larger one. The – sign can be explained in various ways but for now, this simple definition will do.

Write '7 take away 4 = 3' on the board. Now write '7 – 4 = 3' underneath and tell the children that the – sign replaces 'take away'. Write five more simple sums on the board using 'take away', then have a child come to the board and rewrite the sum using the minus sign. Now have the class recite the new version as both '7 minus 4 equals 3' and '7 take away 4 equals 3'. Repeat this with the other examples.

Ask eight children to stand at the front of the class. Say that you are going to take away one of them. Ask how that sum could be written on the board. Write '8 – 1' on the board and have the children read the sentence so far. Expect to hear 'take away' and 'minus' being used. Have one child sit down and complete the number sentence with '= 7'. Now ask two children to sit down and repeat the exercise.

The important point is to have the children become familiar with seeing the – sign and mentally interpreting it as the subtraction operation.

Make two sets of simple cards, one showing the – sign and the other the = sign. Give the cards to pairs of children along with cubes and counters. The more able children might be given plastic coins. One child in each pair must create one number sentence which correctly uses the – and = signs. The other child must check the sum for accuracy and say the sentence in at least two forms using 'minus' and 'take away'. The children then swap roles.

Once the – sign has become part of the class vocabulary, move on to using it with a symbol to represent an unknown number. Similar work should already have taken place with addition. Write an example on the board such as 6 – 4 = ☐. Tell the children that they must work out the mystery number. Ask how they can do it. Expect and encourage different strategies, such as using objects to represent the sets and removing equally until an empty set is achieved, counting on from 4 to 6 or working backwards from 6 on a number line. Even very young children must realise that different methods exist for solving problems.

Points to watch

The less able children being confused by the variety of the strategies.

Resources

Cards showing – and = signs; cubes and counters; plastic coins

Next step

Putting oral or written questions into number sentences using symbols when recording mental calculations.

Recording calculations using symbols

Learning outcome

To use the + and – signs to record mental addition and subtraction in number sentences (Y2)

Assumed knowledge and experience

The children should have worked with the + and – signs. They should also know some of the vocabulary associated with the two operations and be aware that mental processes may be recorded in mathematical formats.

Mathematical importance

Recording mental processes forces the children to be clear about what they are trying to do. It also helps them to interpret a problem and reduce it to a mathematical construct that can be dealt with.

Activities

The children will have carried out similar exercises to these when addition and subtraction were being introduced but the emphasis is now on calculations where the children have to decide which operation needs to be employed and in laying out that calculation correctly. Tell the children that you want them to think about how to solve a problem. Use two boxes, one containing three objects, the other containing two. Have a child take out the three objects and hold them up; ask another child to hold up the two objects from the other box.

Ask the children what sum they would have to do to work out how many there were altogether. Remind them that you do not want the answer itself. Expect suggestions which include 'add' or 'plus'. Tell the class that to find the total you would add. Ask what sign we use for add. Ask how this sum would look if it were written down. Most children will say the larger number first but ask the children if it matters with addition sums. Proceed to writing the number sentence '3 + 2' and ask what sign is used to show where the answer goes. Write in the = sign. Now ask them to give the total; write in '5'. Place different numbers of objects in the boxes.

Give out books to record the mental process but whiteboards would be better. Tell the children that you are going to take the objects out but you do not want them to find the total, but to think about how they would write down this sum. They should not write the sum at this point. After a short while, ask them what sort of sum this is. Expect 'addition' to be mentioned. Ask the children what numbers are involved. Expect them to say the correct numbers. Ask them how they show where the answer goes. Expect them to mention the = sign. Write in the digits, the + sign and the = sign at random positions on the board. Now tell the children to write down what the sum should look like. The whiteboards can be held up by everyone and you can quickly see if the task has been achieved. If whiteboards are being used, highlight those that have put the larger number first or second. It is good to encourage placing the larger number first.

Repeat similar exercises with subtraction. Hold up six objects, put your hands into the box and drop two of them. Ask the children if you now have more or fewer objects. Ask them how they could work out the actual number. Do not let them say the answer. Ask what sort of sum might help to work out the answer. They are likely to say 'subtraction' or 'taking away' but be aware that adding on from 4 to 6 is a perfectly valid strategy. Assuming subtraction, ask them for the figures and the signs that are involved and write them on the board. Ask the children to write down the sum. This time, look especially for children who have placed the larger number second.

Points to watch

Not being able to sort out the appropriate operation.

Resources

Two boxes; individual whiteboards

Next step

Recording more complex mental calculations.

Using symbols in number sentences

Learning outcome

To recognise the use of symbols to stand for unknown numbers in number sentences (Y1 and Y2)

Assumed knowledge and experience

The children should be used to simple symbols such as ? and ☐ to indicate an unknown number (Y1). They should be able to read a number sentence and work the required operation. They should have experience with using symbols when either adding or subtracting.

Mathematical importance

The children need to understand that a symbol may represent an unknown number in any part of the sentence, not just in the answer position.

Activities

Tell the children that they are going to try to find mystery numbers and that you want them each to design a symbol of their own which will represent their unknown number. Only give them a minute for this exercise. Divide the class into pairs and give each pair a +, – and = sign. Write a number sentence on the board that shows the mystery number in the answer position. Illustrate your example with an interesting or amusing symbol for the answer. Have each child make a number sentence for their partner that uses their own symbols. Most children should be able to write the numbers by now but less able children might need LSA support and objects to help them. Encourage the more able children to use numbers which total up to 100. On discovering the mystery number, the children can reverse their roles.

The above activity can be taken further by introducing number sentences where the mystery number is in the sum element, for example, 27 – ☐ = 18. It is worth discussing strategies for this type of problem before starting. Number lines or number squares may be suggested; counting on from 18 to 27 is another alternative and some children may be at the stage of adding 2 to 18 to make 20 and then the 7, giving the answer 9. Encourage the main group and more able children to use different strategies but make sure the less able children are secure with one method.

As a follow-on activity, give oral or written questions that contain an unknown number, for example, 'I think of a number, take away 7 and am left with 12. What number did I first think of?'. Have the children invent a symbol for this unknown number and discuss how the problem may be solved. Write the number sentence as it develops, for example, X – 7 = 12. Ask if the children think the unknown number will be bigger or smaller than 7 and to give their reasons. Repeat this activity with different situations.

Use two different symbols to develop more complex questions, for example, ☐ + △ = 20. Tell the children that each symbol represents a different number. Ask them to verbalise the sentence with phrasing such as 'A number added to a different number equals 20'. Write that number pair on the board and ask for a different pair. Let the children work out other pairs. The 'answer' number may be smaller or larger depending on ability. This work leads neatly into number patterns and the class should be encouraged to look at number sentence arrays such as: 10 + 0 = 10; 9 + 1 = 10; 8 + 2 = 10.

Points to watch

Difficulty in realising which operation is required.

Resources

Cards showing +, – and =

Next step

Similar work with numbers into hundreds.

Addition/subtraction as inverse operations

Learning outcome

To understand that addition and subtraction are inverse operations (Y1)

Assumed knowledge and experience

The children should have a good knowledge of the effect of addition and subtraction. They should be familiar with expressing addition and subtraction problems orally and in writing and using a wide selection of words and phrases.

Mathematical importance

Children need to understand that addition reverses subtraction. This will lead to later work where division will be seen as the inverse of multiplication.

Activities

Write a simple sum on the board, such as $4 + 2 =$ and have the children tell you the answer. Now reverse the numbers and ask if $2 + 4$ also equals 6. Ask the general question whether or not reversing the numbers in addition sums makes any difference. Now write '$6 - 4 =$' and ask for the answer. Next write '$6 - 2 =$' and ask for the answer. Write on the board the four different sums that use 2, 4, and 6. Write three new numbers on the board, such as 8, 5 and 3. Ask the children to suggest a sum which uses these three numbers, for example, $8 - 5 = 3$. Ask for alternatives. Be careful if a sum is given which produces a negative answer, for example, $3 - 8$. The move into negative numbers is very important but needs to be dealt with at a different point.

When the children have produced four sentences for this combination of numbers, for example, $3 + 5 = 8$, $5 + 3 = 8$, $8 - 5 = 3$, $8 - 3 = 5$, put other groups of three digits on the board and ask the children to write sets of appropriate sums. The more able children should be able to deal with number bonds to at least 20. Less able children may still need counters.

Give the children a series of oral questions that will encourage them to think about addition and subtraction being the inverse of each other – questions such as: 'Mary had fifteen oranges but lost some and now only has eight. How many did she lose?', 'David took six cards to school but came home with nine. How many did he gain?'

Through discussion of such problems, bring out various ways of looking at solutions and writing them.

Give each table a set of cards that say either 'true' or 'false'. Give out an activity sheet containing various sums, most of which are true but some of which are false, such as, $9 + 4 = 13$, $6 - 10 = 4$, $21 = 9 + 12$, $14 - 3 = 11$.

Have the children copy out each sum and write either true or false alongside it. Although copying out sums of this type may sometimes be a waste of time, for this activity it will help to reinforce the idea of importance of position.

Points to watch

Children who subtract the larger number from the smaller without realising they have introduced negative numbers.

Resources

Counters; true/false cards

Next step

The inverse nature of addition and subtraction with numbers to 1000.

Checking results

We all make mistakes when making calculations. Even the widespread use of calculators has not stopped mistakes occurring, especially when incorrect numbers are inputted. Methods of checking calculations are very important and begin with infants. The strategies at that age are very restricted of course but nevertheless very important for two reasons. Firstly, children need to get into the habit of being accurate. This will enable success in future work and reinforce processes. Secondly, checking for accuracy by using different methods indicates that more than one strategy is known and these will be of great benefit in later years. Diverse strategies need to be developed over time but are always a sign of a good mathematician.

Addition in Key Stage 1 may be checked in a number of ways. Some children, probably the less able ones, may wish to either continue with counters and 3-D objects to help them or, more likely, return to the use of solid equipment as a checking device. Others may find number lines or number squares useful tools. A good method of checking, for children starting to be confident with numbers, is to simply add the numbers in a different order. This is a very good method especially with lists of three or more numbers or amounts.

Subtraction can also be checked in a variety of ways. If the initial calculation has been straightforward, for example, $17 - 9 = 8$, using seventeen objects and removing nine could check this. It might also be checked by making one group of seventeen objects and another of nine and removing one from each until an empty group appears. A number line or number square may be used to count backwards from 17 in ones. Counting on from 9 to 17 may also check the calculation. Children should know all of these strategies although, by the end of Key Stage 1, they should be starting to have a preferred method.

Above all, children must learn to use common sense and their knowledge of the number system and order when checking; if 6 has been added to 7 and the answer is 89, something has gone badly wrong! Thus common sense, allied with simple work on approximation, can work wonders before more formal strategies are used.

Addition in different order/Checking

Learning outcome

To check an answer by adding in a different order or by using an equivalent calculation (Y2)

Assumed knowledge and experience

The children should have a knowledge of number names and order to at least 100. They should be able to add and subtract mentally and know the number bonds to at least 20. They should realise that addition can be done in any order but not subtraction. They should be able to do addition and subtraction in written form using symbols.

Mathematical importance

Mathematical calculations almost always need to be checked, even when a calculator is used. Children need simple techniques to enable checking for accuracy.

Activities

Remind the children that addition may be done in any order. Show a few examples on the board that contain at least three numbers or amounts. Shopping lists like the following would be very useful:

Fizzers 24p
Gobstoppers 12p
Bubble gum 50p

Eraser 21p
Pencil 35p
Ruler 42p

Add the first list from top to bottom to begin with but deliberately miscount and write an incorrect total. So much the better if a child picks up your 'error'. Now check the answer by adding from bottom to top. A different total! A mistake has been made! Now check the top to bottom addition again and see if agreement can be reached. Try the second list and the children will probably be paying a great deal of attention! Give the children lots of practice with lists of three or more amounts. These examples deliberately show the additions in vertical form although it is not introduced until Year 3 in the NNS.

Nevertheless, lists are normally written vertically and it would be pointless to waste a realistic opportunity.

Check a subtraction sum with a number line. Place a finger on the number line in the position of the right-hand number in the sum and count on the number given in the answer. Does it match the left-hand figure in the sum?

Tell the class that you think 15 take away 7 is 9. Ask the class for different ways your answer could be checked. Have children either explain their methods verbally while you write on the board or have the children write the methods themselves. Involve the rest of the class by asking if they agree.

This activity is more likely to be used by the main group and the more able children. Remind the children that addition reverses the subtraction process. Given a sum, such as $12 - 5 = 7$, tell them that by adding the numbers either side of the = sign, they should reach the first number. Give some examples to work out where the answer to the original sum is deliberately incorrect. Can they spot it by checking?

Points to watch

Children using checking procedures inaccurately.

Resources

Books or whiteboards

Next step

Checking halving with doubling and multiplication with division.

Rapid recall

This work is very closely related to mental arithmetic but should not be confused. Where mental arithmetic is often about methods of calculation and learning strategies, rapid recall is just that, memorising facts about numbers and connections between them. Rapid recall assists mental arithmetic. It is rather like learning to lay bricks before building walls; once the basic skill is in place, the various ways of connecting the bricks can be experimented with and developed.

At the heart of this work is a recognition that children must be able to recognise numbers in all forms, know their order and their relationships to each other. Number lines are very useful in this work but the visual array of number squares is even more helpful. The children will see patterns in the number, recognise where they exist in relation to each other and begin to see connections. The 2×, 5× and 10× tables are central to this work as are doubling and halving skills. This work is often covered in the NNS through the opening 'warm up' session and children usually enjoy it. Remember to use targeted differentiated questioning so that all abilities are involved and learning.

Use as many stimuli as possible; number squares, lines and sticks are very good for the main groups and the more able children but the less able children are likely to need concrete materials such as coins and counters.

As with other maths for children at this age, try to relate the learning to 'real life' problems. Find out how much pocket money they receive and ask them how much doubling it would make. Have displays of two, five and ten numbers in the classroom, school and at home. Highlight dates that are even – when was half that date, when will double that date be?

Rapid recall means just that. The hope is that children will know these number facts instantaneously and many will. Others will take more time and a few may never be quick. Timing the children can be good fun as long as the less able ones do not become dispirited. Timing in pairs is good if they can use a stopwatch. Class lists showing speeds usually motivate some but can be cruel for others.

Number pairs totalling ten/bond bingo

Learning outcome

To know by heart all number pairs with a total of ten (Y1) and a total of twenty (Y2)

Assumed knowledge and experience

The children should have a good knowledge of number names to at least 20. They should be familiar with the concept of addition and counting on. They should be able to use a number line for counting.

Mathematical importance

Knowing the number bonds to 10 and 20, so that they may be recalled almost immediately, is a great asset when performing more complex operations.

Activities

Improving speed of recall will come with increasing familiarity with the number bonds. Increasing speed should be aimed for in all the following activities.

The coconut shy activity. Sit ten children at the front of the class in two groups of five. Give out one set of cards to each group that shows the numbers 1–5. To begin with, the children hold the cards in number order from left to right. Now the children put the cards face down on their laps. Tell the children in the groups that when you tap them on the shoulder they have to stand up and display their card to the rest of the class. The rest of the class have to total the numbers as they appear. Go to the left-hand group and touch a shoulder. Walk to the right-hand group and do the same thing. Two numbers are now displayed and the children should give their answers. After a little while, increase the speed at which you move between the groups. Pretend to become out of breath as you move more and more quickly. Change the children holding the cards and repeat the exercise. Play a similar game using cards showing 1–10 for number bonds to 20. As a variation, jumble the cards so that they are not in order.

How many bonds? Hold up a card that shows a number from 1 to 10/20. Children should name one bond that gives that number. Ask the children for another bond for the same number. Insist on speed. Ensure the slowest children have a chance to answer at some point.

Bond bingo. The preparation for this will take a few minutes. Make some bingo-type cards which instead of showing numbers, show the number bonds (see Activity sheet 43) to 10. Give the cards out to individuals or groups, possibly of the less able children. Now make a show of removing a card from a bag or hat. Each card shows a number from 2 to 10. If children are familiar and comfortable with 0, this may also be included and the number cards should go from 1 to 10. Play bingo in the traditional way with children spotting any of the number bonds on their cards which match the numbers being called.

Points to watch

Children who are flustered by the need to recall at speed. Some children may never learn rapid recall but at least they might become quick!

Resources

Number cards showing 1–5; number cards showing 1–10; bingo cards and counters

Next step

Subtraction facts to 10.

Multiples of 10 totalling 100

Learning outcome

To recall rapidly all pairs of multiples of 10 to a total of 100 (Y2)

Assumed knowledge and experience

The children should know the meaning of 'multiples'. They should be able to use number lines to count on and back in tens. They should have a good knowledge of the numbers and the number order to 100. They should know that a symbol may be used to represent a missing number.

Mathematical importance

This is another useful tool in assisting with mental calculations, for example, when adding 23 and 56, being able to immediately know that 20 and 50 equals 70 is helpful.

Activities

Tens snap. Make sets of cards that show all the multiples of 10p up to 90p, at least three of each card per set. Give sets out to pairs of children and tell them to shuffle the packs. The children will then play snap with a slight difference. First go through the rules of ordinary snap where each child turns over a card in turn and when two are cards with the same value are placed on top of each other, the first person to call 'Snap!' wins the pile. Play this for a little while to ensure they are all used to the rules. Now tell them to reshuffle the cards. Explain the rules of tens snap. Play begins with one person putting down a card followed by the other child. 'Snap!' is called if the values of the two cards add up to exactly 100p. The winner takes the pile for their own. Although making these cards may seem like a lot of work, they have many uses throughout the infant and junior years and if laminated, will last for a long time.

Stand up for 100. Make yourself some A4 cards that show the multiples of 10 to 90. Have each child write a number for themself that is also a multiple of 10. Writing on whiteboards would be preferable if they are available. Tell the children that you are going to become a tens number and if they can help you become a hundreds number they must hold up their card. Shuffle your cards and draw one at random.

Hold it up to show the class. Children who have the complementary card to make a total of 100 should hold up their number. Have any children who have held up their card show their cards around and gain general agreement that the solutions are correct. If wrong cards are held up, quickly correct mistakes. Also look out for children who should have held up their cards but did not. Repeat this several times. Allow a child to take your place and observe the children as they work out if their card should be held up. This is a useful assessment opportunity and should lead to giving assistance to any children who do not understand the idea.

Missing multiples! This activity is more formal. Write number sentences that display the answer and one multiple of 10 but not the other multiple. The missing multiple can be represented by a symbol, for example, $60 + \boxed{} = 100$, $\boxed{} + 30 = 100$. The children must work out the missing multiple and write it in the square.

Since this work revolves around developing speed, have the children work in pairs and time themselves using a stopwatch. The children have to write down the multiple pairs which total 100 as fast as they can. This should be done once at the beginning of the work and once towards the end.

Points to watch

Less able children who are unable to read and say the number names to 100.

Resources

Stopwatch; tens snap cards; number cards showing 10–90

Next step

Pairs of multiples of 5 that total 100.

Addition doubles and halves to 10

Learning outcome

To know addition doubles and halves of all numbers to 10 (Y1 and Y2)

Assumed knowledge and experience

The children should have confidence in using, reading and saying the numbers to at least 20. They should be able to use a number line and number square to help recognition and ordering skills. They should have awareness of addition and subtraction as a process and possibly recognition of the + and − signs.

Mathematical importance

Doubling and halving offers the facility to calculate quickly with the four operations and is very helpful in work with multiplication tables that comes later.

Activities

Ask the children what they think 'double' means. Discuss definitions and use objects to represent what is happening. Doubling may be thought of as 'twice as much' or 'adding the same amounts together'. Children should quickly understand that doubling means 'two lots of'.

This activity requires the children to sit in a circle. Objects should be scattered around the floor inside the circle; small balls would be good. Pick up one ball and tell the children you are going to play tennis and need double that number. Ask how many double one is. One child picks up two balls and comes to you. Tell the children that the child has double your number of balls: you have one but the child has two. Now say that another child needs double that number to play catch. Ask how many they should have. Another child picks up four balls and comes to the centre. Repeat this with four doubled to eight. Finally, double eight.

Before the lesson, write on the board 'double 1 is ?', 'double 2 is ?', 'double 4 is ?' and 'double 8 is ?'. Now ask the children to help you complete the sentences. Go back to the ball activity and this time select three balls, then six. Write on the board 'double 3 is?' and 'double 6 is?'. Repeat with 5 and 10 being doubled and complete with 7 and 9. The board should show a list of the number doubles to 10. The children should rewrite the list in the correct order.

Discuss the terms 'half of' and 'halving'. Agree that halving is sharing into two equal groups or amounts. Using objects like PE balls, take two and say you are going to give half to a friend. Ask the children how many you should give. Put the balls into two equal groups and tell the children that half of 2 is 1. Repeat by halving 4, 6, 8 and 10. Write the number sentences on the board and have children say them. As an important teaching point, before going any further, ask the children 'If half of 4 is 2, what is double 2?'. The main group and the more able children should come to know that halving and doubling are inverse operations. Complete the activity with the other halves of even numbers to 20.

Use Activity sheet 45 that states five times 'Double ___ is ___'. 'Half of ___ is ___.' Use two boxes or bags, one containing numbers from 1 to 10, the other containing the even numbers to 20. Remove in turn numbers at random from each bag or box. The numbers from the 1–10 bag must be doubled while those from the other bag should be halved. Children should write their answers on the activity sheets. Repeat this exercise as often as necessary.

Use opportunities during the day to put this into 'real life' contexts; for example, 'The date is the 18th. What is half of 18?', 'Six children are on the blue table. What is double 6?'.

Points to watch

Not remembering the doubles/halves of the larger numbers.

Resources

PE balls; numbers 1–10 on card; even numbers to 20 on card; two bags or boxes

Next step

Doubling to 15 and doubling multiples of 5.

Subtraction facts to 10

Learning outcome

To begin to know subtraction facts to at least 10 (Y1)

Assumed knowledge and experience

The children should understand the operation of subtraction and the vocabulary associated with it. They should begin to understand that subtracting or adding 0 leaves a number unchanged. They should know that a symbol can represent an unknown number.

Mathematical importance

Rapid recall of basic facts is all-important in later work that relies on accurate and quick response; for example, mental subtraction to 100.

Activities

The children may already be acquainted with the operation of subtraction and have written number sentences. These exercises are intended to make the children more familiar with the number bonds and thus enable greater speed.

The children should work in pairs. Timers or stopwatches would be very useful. Give one of the children a pack of 1–10 cards. Have the cards shuffled and placed face down on the table. Tell the children that when they start, a card will be shown and they must subtract that number from 10 and say the answer. The card-picking child picks them up one at a time and shows each one quickly to the other child who must answer as quickly as possible. When the cards have all gone, the timer can be stopped and the time recorded. The timing may be a bit difficult for younger children but some may be able to try it. The exercise could also be done with an adult helper who could time four or five children at the same time.

The same activity may be done with any target number up to 10.

Give the children a selection of plastic coins with the values 1p, 2p, 5p and 10p. Tell the children that you

are going to call out an amount and they must subtract that amount from 10p. They then have to make up that amount as quickly as they can, using the coins. Use the same exercise with different amounts.

Give the children a selection of questions which include a symbol to represent a missing number, for example, $8 - \square = 5$, $10 - \square = 1$, $4 - \square = 0$. The questions should be differentiated for ability groups. Tell the class that you are going to clap your hands slowly ten times and they must complete the sums before the tenth clap. Repeat the activity a few times, then give a different selection of sums and only clap nine times. As long as the questions are well differentiated, the slower children should not become discouraged if they do not complete the work.

Have the children working in pairs. One child must ask their partner to write down all the subtraction pairs for 3; for example, $3 - 3 = 0$, $3 - 2 = 1$, $3 - 1 = 2$ and $3 - 0 = 3$. The other child then names a different number and repeats the exercise. This continues until all the numbers have been used. The children then swap answer sheets and check each other's work.

Points to watch

Speed not increasing, especially with less able children.

Resources

Timers or stopwatches; 1–10 cards

Next step

Addition and subtraction facts to 20.

Number bonds to 10 (+ and –)

Learning outcome

To know by heart all addition and subtraction facts for each number to at least 10 (Y2)

Assumed knowledge and experience

The children should understand the operations of addition and subtraction and the vocabulary associated with them. They should also understand that subtracting or adding 0 leaves a number unchanged. They should know that a symbol can represent an unknown number and use this to solve simple problems.

Mathematical importance

A firm grasp of the number bonds to 10 and beyond greatly assists quick calculation.

Activities

The children can work in pairs. Give each pair a dice. One child throws the dice and they both record the number with a + sign. The other child then throws the dice; they record the number and write the answer after an = sign. It is possible with a normal 1–6 dice that the totals 11 and 12 might be achieved. In most cases in Year 2, this should not be seen as a problem. Children of this age should be able to deal with 11 and 12. If some children have the objective of dealing with only 10, the 6 on the dice may be taped over and considered as a 0.

The children should continue throwing the dice and recording the sums produced but warn them that the same number combination is likely to come up more than once. When this happens, they can write the sum down again or place a tick against the sum every time it happens. This leads neatly into ways of recording for data handling exercises. It is very likely that the same numbers will also be thrown but in different orders, for example, 4 + 5 and 5 + 4. This situation is worth discussing. The children should know that the order of addition does not affect the result but you may want to consider it as a 'different' sum for the purpose of this activity.

A similar game to the one above can be played individually. The children simply write down '10 –' and throw the dice, record the number next to the minus sign and complete the answer. This will only produce a limited number of results and so the total can be moved up to 11 or 12 for those who are secure at 10.

Using coloured connecting cubes, ask the children to make a 3-D display of the number bonds to 10. They could start with a 'rod' or 'stick' of ten pinks, then nine pinks and one green, and so on. This can be formalised in written form with 10 + 0 = 10, 9 + 1 = 10. This could become part of a display in the maths area.

Repeat the exercise with the equivalent subtractions but this time with the green cubes separated by a small gap from the pink cubes.

With small variations, all of the above activities may be undertaken using a number other than 10, 11 or 12 as the target. Some computer programs contain similar work to that above and the Internet contains a great deal of material on this subject.

Calculators do not have the same importance at Key Stage 1 in the NNS as they did previously but good use may be made of them in checking answers in these activities.

Points to watch

Speed of recall not being increased.

Resources

Some track games may be suitable; 1–6 dice; calculators

Next step

Number bonds to 20.

2× and 10× tables

Learning outcome

To know by heart multiplication facts for 2× and 10× tables (Y2)

Assumed knowledge and experience

The children should have experience of counting on exercises using a number line, particularly with twos and tens. They should understand multiplication as repeated addition. They should have experience of work on doubling.

Mathematical importance

Being able to access this information accurately and quickly enables more complicated procedures to be undertaken with more certainty and at a faster rate.

Activities

Begin by revising counting on in twos using a standard number line. Insist on speed. Draw a number line from 0 to 20 with marks showing the unit positions but not the numbers. Repeat the exercise and set the speed by pointing at the appropriate marks as you move along the line towards 20. After a few times, reverse direction and have the children count backward in twos from 20. Do the same exercises with various groups such as boys, girls, tables and differentiated ability groups.

Use a number stick divided into ten sections (see page 101).

In this activity, the numbers of the 'times tables' should be indicated as going from left to right as the children see it. Tell the children that each section represents two. Hold the stick horizontally and tell the children that the end of the stick on the left represents no twos. Ask how many no twos there are. Go to the first section and say this shows one lot of twos and ask how much this is. Go to the second section and say 'this is two twos, how much is this?'. Now count up from 0 in twos to 20. Go to the right end of the stick and tell the children this represents ten twos; ask how many that represents. Ask a child to point at the centre of the stick. Ask how many twos this shows. When they say 'five twos', ask them

to tell you what five twos are. Now repeat starting from 0 but introduce as 'one lot of twos is', 'two lots of two are' and go up to 'five lots of two are'. Stop after five twos and write on the board the table so far in the form '1 lot of twos are 2', '2 lots of 2 are 4' and continue to '5 lots of 2 are 10'.

The next activity will complete the twos by using doubling knowledge. Have a quick warm up with the stick going from no twos to five twos. Ask what ten twos are. Point out that ten twos are double five twos. Ask if they can work out by doubling what six twos will be. They should be thinking that six twos will be double three twos. When this is established, move on to eight twos being double four twos. Work with the number stick on the one, two, three, four, five, six, eight and ten twos. Write these on the board and ask what's missing. Using the number stick ask them what six twos are and eight twos. Ask them if they can they work out what seven twos are. Use the same idea with nine twos. Once the table has been established orally, use the number stick to recite the twos in order using 'one lot of twos is 2, two lots of two are 4'. After that, start to pick out particular parts of the table, building on the easier examples but making sure the 7 and 9 are also covered adequately. Repeat similar work with the 10× table.

Points to watch

Children having difficulty picking up speed beyond six twos.

Resources

Blank number line; 0–20 number line; number stick

Next step

Secure knowledge of 2× and 10× and beginnings of 5× tables.

Multiplication facts for 5× table

Learning outcome

To begin to know multiplication facts for 5× table up to 5 × 10 (Y2)

Assumed knowledge and experience

The children should have experience of counting on exercises using a number line. They should be able to look for patterns on a 1–100 square, especially with the multiples of 5. they should have experience of work on doubling and should know that multiplication can be looked on as repeated addition.

Mathematical importance

Easily accessing all multiplication tables helps to facilitate more complex calculations. The 5× table works as an important link between the 2× and 10× tables.

Activities

Ask the children to look at a number square and tell you any numbers they can see that end in 5. As they are said, mark the numbers off. Now ask the children to count on five from 5. Mark off the 10. Now do the same from 15. Mark off 20. Ask if five on from 25 will be 30. Mark off 30. Generalise and ask if five on from a '5 number' will always end in 0. See if it works with 35 and 85. Mark off all the numbers ending in 0. Tell the children that numbers that end in 5 and 0 are part of what we call the 5× table. Tell them that this is the set of numbers made when we count in steps of five from 0. Have the children recite the multiples of 5 up to 50 as you point to the appropriate places on the number square. Repeat forwards and backwards with different groups of children so that they become familiar with the group of number names and the order.

Use a number stick in the same way as described on page 54. The work will follow a similar pattern with the introduction of one, two, three, four, five and ten, followed by the others. Record them on the board using 'one lot of five is 5', 'two lots of 5 are 10' and so on.

Give out plastic coins with the values 5p and 10p. Have the children each make a small chart showing '1 lot of 5p is' and have the children draw quickly around a 5p and label it. Repeat this up to ten lots

of 5p but the children should use 10ps for the multiples of 10; for example, two 10ps for 20p and a combination of one 5p and the appropriate number of 10ps for the rest.

Make sets of cards showing multiples of 5 to 50 (see *Blueprints Maths Key Stage* 1: *Pupil Resource Book* page 94). Give these out to children and have them work on them in pairs. The set of cards needs to be shuffled. One child takes a card from the top and reads out the number while the other child has to say how many lots of 5 that represents. After the pack has been gone through once, the roles are reversed and the game continues.

The less able children may be given the 5–50 number cards. Tell them to place these in order without referring to a number line or number square.

Give each child a number fan that shows the multiples of 5. Ask the whole class fairly formal multiplication table questions along the lines of 'What are three fives?' and 'How many fives are the same as 45?'. Although number fans can slow things down a bit for the most able children, they can help to reinforce the number order for the main group and the less able children. The more able ones may be able to complete written questions during this session.

Points to watch

The less able children only picking up on the lower numbers.

Resources

Number stick; 1–100 number square; marker pen; 5p and 10p coins; 5–50 cards set

Next step

Secure knowledge and rapid recall of 2×, 5× and 10× tables.

Division, 2×, 10× tables/10-multiples halves

Learning outcome

To know division facts for 2× and 10× tables (Y2)

To know halves of multiples of 10 to 100 (Y2)

Assumed knowledge and experience

The children should have some experience of working with the 2× and 10× tables. They should have an understanding of the multiples of 10, probably using a number line and number square. The children should know that subtraction reverses the operation of addition.

Mathematical importance

Children need to realise as early as possible that multiplication and division are very closely linked and by knowing one set of information, for example, the multiplication tables, division problem solving can become simpler.

Activities

This work is related to the children being able to rapidly recall the division facts for the 2× and 10× tables. Although it is clearly linked to the working of division problems, that process is not taught here.

Using a number line and a 1–100 number square, quickly revise the 2× and 10× tables. Write the 2× table on the board in the traditional way starting with $1 \times 2 = 2$ at the top and going down to $10 \times 2 = 20$ at the bottom. Highlight the $3 \times 2 = 6$ line. Draw six simple shapes like sweets on the board. Ask the children to share the 'sweets' equally between two children. Ask how many they would each receive. Write on the board '6 shared by 2 is 3'. Now ask how many 'sweets' each one would have if three children shared them. Write up '6 shared by 3 is 2'. Show the children the $3 \times 2 = 6$ sum and the two 'shared' sentences. Ask if they notice anything. Start them thinking about the same numbers being involved.

Tell them that just as addition and subtraction are inverse operations, so are multiplication and division. Repeat the exercise with $5 \times 2 = 10$, 10 shared by 2 is 5 and 10 shared by 5 is 2. Now begin to abstract and write '$4 \times 2 = 8$' on the board. Ask if anyone can tell you what 8 shared by 4 is. Continue until the children begin to see the connection. Most children

will pick up the idea quickly but the less able ones may need concrete materials to help them.

Write the 2× and 10× tables on the board. Give the children activity sheets that contain rows of the same sentence: _____ shared by _____ is _____ . The children must convert each part of the tables into their division equivalents, for example, 50 shared by 10 is 5.

Give out 2p plastic coins to the children. Working in pairs, one child takes a handful of 2ps and counts them. They then tell the other child how much they have and the other child has to write down how many 2p coins they have. Repeat this with 10p coins.

For halves of multiples of 10 to 100, use a number stick. Have the children count on from 0 to 100 as you point to the divisions on the number stick. Point to 20. Ask what number is halfway between 0 and 20. Repeat with 40. Then go to half of 100. Move on to 60 and 80. Write these on the board in order to leave gaps between them for the odd multiples. Ask what half of 10 is. Now ask for half of 30. Discuss what is happening as needs be or use a number square to help. On completion, write up on board the remainder of the halves.

Points to watch

Inability to read the inverse information from the tables.

Resources

Number stick; 1–100 number square; 2p and 10p coins

Next step

Use known facts to aid mental and written strategies.

Doubles to 15/doubles of multiples of 5

Learning outcome

To know the doubles of all numbers to at least 15 (Y2)

To know the doubles of all multiples of 5 to 50 (Y2)

Assumed knowledge and experience

The children should know the doubles of all numbers to 10. They should understand that doubling means totalling two groups of the same number or amount.

They should know the multiples of 5 to 50, probably through use of a number line or number square. They should understand that a symbol can represent an unknown number.

Mathematical importance

Doubling is a useful skill in its own right but takes on even greater importance when allied to mental arithmetic strategies.

Activities

Remind the children of how they doubled the numbers from 1 to 10. Show a picture of a football team and ask how many players are on each team. Write 11 on the board. Ask how many there are in two teams. Write '11 + 11', '11 × 2' and '22' on the board. Now ask how many months there are in a year – some Year 2 children should know. Write '12' on the board. Ask how many months there are in two years. Write '12 + 12', '12 × 2' and '24' on the board. Now ask if they can see how they went from 11 to 22 and from 12 to 24. Show them that by doubling each digit they have arrived at the whole double. Ask if they can quickly tell you what double 13 and double 14 are. Write these doubles on the board. Now ask if they can tell you the double of 15. Care needs to be taken at this point because someone may want to say 210, representing double 1 and double 5. If this does happen, ask them to think about 15 as 10 and 5. First double 10 and then double 5, then add them both together: 30!

Make a set of snap cards, each showing, for example, either 'double 12', '12 + 12' or '12 × 2'. Also make another set showing the doubles themselves, 22, 24, 26, 28 and 30. One child of a pair has the 'question' cards and lays out one at a time while the other child has to find the correct double. After each round, swap the cards.

Produce a set of activity sheets or cards that show written sums such as 13 + ☐ = 26. The children must complete each question. They will soon pick up that they just need to repeat the given number so change the questions for the main group and the more able children to ☐ + ☐ = 30, for example, but tell the children that when the symbol is the same it means that both missing numbers are the same.

For the children to learn the doubles of the multiples of 5, begin by using a number square. Point to 5 and ask them to double it. Tell them this means two lots of five or counting on five from 5. Now ask them to double 10. Use the number square to show that doubling 10 gives 20. Reinforce this by doubling 10p to make 20p. Write this information on the board: 'Double 5 is 10', 'Double 10 is 20'.

Now ask them what they think double 15 is. Remind them of the two doubles already on the board. They should realise that double 15 will be the same as the sum of double 10 and double 5. Move on to double 20. Once again, they may realise that doubling 2 will give 4 so doubling 20 will give 40. Ask if they can double 25. Remind them that this is the same as double 20 add double 5. Double 30 should be okay now and double 35 will follow. Complete to double 50. Use 5p and 10p coins to perform practical doubling and have the children convert two 5ps into a 10p when appropriate.

Points to watch

Although doubling each digit is a crude method, it will help doubling to a certain level.

Next step

Doubling numbers up to 100.

Resources

Doubling snap cards; 1–100 number squares

Multiplication and division

Most teachers believe that the operations of multiplication and division are the first real tests of a child's abilities to deal with number. It is true that some children stumble with subtraction but these two operations need to be tackled very carefully. For this reason, the National Numeracy Strategy has included lots of preparatory work that should help to provide good number knowledge before the formal multiplication and division methods are taught. The children should be used to 'reading' numbers and number sentences in various forms. They should have experience with number lines and number squares and have carried out work with halving and doubling procedures. All the experiences provided to this point should help them have a clear idea of the ways in which numbers are related. Familiarity with the numbers to 100 is essential.

The operation of multiplication should be looked on as repeated addition. This is not a new concept and multiplication has been taught through this device for many years. What has changed in many schools is the way in which children are now expected to understand and develop the knowledge through lots of mental practice and rapid recall exercises rather than completing pages of sums. In the past, some children have simply moved straight into formal written methods. Children need to be given lots of work to reinforce the multiplication idea but care needs to be taken to differentiate between children who have understood the process and those who have not. If the process is understood, repeated practice of pages of sums is not necessary. If the process is not understood, other explanatory methods need to be used of which extra practice may be one.

The same applies to division where, arguably, even more care needs to be taken. Division may be thought of as repeated subtraction but is generally taught as sharing equally. This is a very reasonable way of explaining division to children and as long as the numbers are kept fairly small and manageable, they will gradually come to understand what division means. The danger is in going too quickly into recording with ever-larger numbers so that struggling with the numbers confuses the process.

When the children are fairly comfortable with each separate operation, it is proper to begin relating them to each other. In the same way as addition and subtraction are inverse operations, so multiplication and division are inverses but very young children who are finding it difficult to hold on to their concepts might struggle, so be gentle!

Multiplication as repeated addition

Learning outcome

To understand multiplication as repeated addition (Y2)

To use and begin to read the related vocabulary (Y2)

Assumed knowledge and experience

The children should have worked with doubling activities and be aware in a general sense of terms such as 'multiply', 'times' and 'lots of'. They should know the meaning of the = sign.

Mathematical importance

Multiplication and division join addition and subtraction to complete the group of four fundamental ways of calculating with number.

Activities

Remind the children that mathematicians like to be a bit clever when they write things down. They do not like to write words if they can help it and often use signs. Tell the children that they are going to be working with multiplication today. Write 'multiplication' on the board. Ask if the children think it is a long word. Tell them that mathematicians have replaced the word multiplication with a simple sign. Draw the × symbol on the board. Now go on to its meaning.

With the class sitting in a circle, place two objects next to each other, then two more objects and then two more. Ask how many objects there are in total; then ask how they worked it out. The children are likely to say that they added two on two on two. Write this down on the board in the form $2 + 2 + 2 = 6$. Now say that we can think of $2 + 2 + 2$ as three lots of 2. Write '3 lots of $2 = 6$' underneath. Repeat the exercise a few times with different numbers of groups and objects but always write it out in the form shown here.

Repeat the activity but insist the children give you the wording correctly, for example, 'five lots of 2 equals 10'. As the children say the words, write them on the board using the = sign. Ask the children if they noticed that you did not write 'equals' but put =

instead. After some examples, tell the children that you are a bit fed up with writing 'lots of' and want to write a symbol instead. Ask if anyone remembers the new sign introduced earlier. Draw the × again and tell the children this represents 'lots of' but sometimes we say 'times' and sometimes 'multiply'.

Give out cubes or counters to each table. The children work in pairs. Have one child make a sum by forming groups of objects on the table. The other child in the pair has to write down the sum in three forms, for example, '$1 + 1 + 1 + 1$', '4 lots of 1', '$4 × 1$'. Now the children reverse roles and repeat the exercise. The main group may miss out the $1 + 1 + 1 + 1$ part. The most able children may be able to just use the $4 × 1$ version and give the answer.

Reverse the whole process and give the children a series of $2 × 4$ type statements. Ask the children to arrange a display with the counters to show what this means. Encourage the children to display the counters in a pattern, for example, $2 × 4$ could be shown as an array of two rows of four counters.

Have the main group and the more able children look at how many different arrays they can make for the same number.

Points to watch

Confusion between the + and × signs with the less able children.

Resources

Counters

Next step

Multiplication can be done in any order. Multiplication in 'real' contexts.

Division as grouping

Learning outcome

To begin to understand division as grouping (repeated subtraction) (Y2)

To use and begin to read the related vocabulary (Y2)

Assumed knowledge and experience

The children should have worked with doubling and halving activities and talked about sharing in a general way. They should also know the meaning of the = sign.

Mathematical importance

Division is the last of the 'big four' operations which form the basis of dealing with numbers at the primary level.

Activities

Have the children sit in a circle. Ask them if they have ever had to share things with other people, maybe a brother or sister. Did sharing cause problems? Were they told to share fairly? Tell them that they are going to be looking at the mathematical way of sharing which is called division. Write 'division' on the board. Tell the children that they will meet another new sign and draw the ÷ symbol on the board. Tell them that is a special sign that means 'division', 'divide' or 'divided by'. For this work, the ÷ sign will stand for 'shared equally by'.

Place six sweets in the centre of the group. Say that you are willing to share your sweets with another child. When the child has been chosen, give the child one sweet and you keep five for yourself. Ask if this was fair. Encourage the children to use the expression 'shared equally' although some children may prefer to think of the operation as 'sharing fairly'. Put the six sweets back together and say that you are now going to share the sweets equally with the child but how many should you each have. Ask 'How many shall we each have?'. The response 'three' should be given by some at least so ask how they worked it out. Demonstrate the equal sharing by giving a sweet to the child then one to yourself and continuing until each of you has three. Ask the children if this is fair. Repeat with other even numbers of sweets being shared by two. Move on to other numbers of sweets being shared by three and so on.

The children now work in pairs. Give out counters or cubes. Tell the children to select one colour that will represent people. The children choose any even number of counters they want and share them equally between the 'people'. Have them divide the counters equally between two 'people' by removing them one at a time from the main pile and giving them to a 'person' until none are left. The children must record their working in the form of, for example, '24 shared equally by 2 is 12'. Keep to even numbers being shared by two for some of the time and the least able children but the rest should move on to other combinations such as multiples of 3 being shared equally by three.

Give out counters or cubes to each group. Have each child select an even number of cubes, for example, twelve. The children must now write their number 'shared equally by 2 is' and complete the answer. Tell the children to write four more number sentences using a different even number of counters each time.

Remind the children that they have seen a new sign that is a quick way of writing 'shared equally by'. Draw it on the board. Now have the children write the same group of number sentences but replacing 'shared equally by' with the ÷ sign.

Points to watch

Children accidentally setting up situations where a remainder might come about.

Resources

Counters and cubes

Next step

Understanding that, for example, 21 ÷ 3 also means 'How many threes make 21?'.

Multiply and divide with confidence

Learning outcome

To use the ×, ÷ and = signs to record mental calculations (Y2)

To recognise the use of a symbol to stand for an unknown number (Y2)

Assumed knowledge and experience

The children should have some experience of working with the ×, ÷ and = signs when beginning formal multiplication and division. They should realise that a symbol can stand for an unknown number.

Mathematical importance

Knowing the ×, ÷ and = signs and how to use them correctly aids the children when they formalise their mental methods. This helps them to think clearly and explain their thought processes.

Activities

Give the children a series of oral questions that centre on mental multiplication. Questions such as:

I have three bags. Each bag holds two bottles. How many bottles do I have?

The car can seat four people. How many people will fit into two cars?

A tube holds ten sweets. How many sweets will there be in five tubes?

How many days in two weeks?

Ask the questions slowly and repeat them at least twice. Do not ask for an answer but tell the children to write down how they could work out the answer. Remind them of the symbols they have been taught. The children should write down their thoughts on paper or whiteboards; whiteboards would be better because they can be immediately held up to show answers. Look for clear thinking and the correct use of symbols. Ensure the children have removed the important factual information, for example, the numbers and required operation, from the wording. At this point, it is worth discussing whether the order of the numbers matters, that is, is 3 × 2 the same as 2 × 3? On completion of the exercise, have the children work out the answers.

For division, follow a similar pattern to that described above but look closely at what happens when the numbers are reversed. Ask the children if reversing the numbers with division makes a difference. At this stage, it is important for children to know that the number order does not matter in multiplication but that it does with division.

Continue this work with an activity that mixes questions between multiplication and division. Sorting out which operation to use is a very important mathematical skill.

Remind the children that a symbol can be used to stand for an unknown number. They were introduced to this idea with addition and subtraction problems. Tell them that a number multiplied by two is six. Ask what the mystery number is. Now write the sum formally like this: ? × 2 = 6. They should work out that the mystery number is 3. Ask the children how they worked it out. It is important that children explain clearly how they think. Some might have known from rapid recall practice that three twos are six. Others might say that three lots of two make six. A few might have worked out that six shared by two is three. These are all legitimate strategies and, at this age, developing strategies is very good.

Points to watch.

A child who cannot decide which is the appropriate operation.

Resources

Whiteboards

Next step

Understanding that division reverses multiplication.

Choosing operations, efficient methods

Learning outcome

To use multiplication and division symbols with confidence (Y2)

Assumed knowledge and experience

The children should recognise the × and ÷ symbols and have used them in solving simple problems, mainly when they have needed to record the results of mental methods.

Mathematical importance

The children have been taught the concepts of multiplication and division but they also need to relate them to problem solving. This will involve use of the symbols in all sorts of contexts and this work is aimed at widening their understanding of the use of the symbols.

Activities

The majority of these activities will be aimed at having the children transform oral or written questions into mathematical symbols. The work should only be undertaken when you have some confidence that the concepts of multiplication and division are well understood. Similar exercises might have been carried out before but this time we are using an extended range of words when asking the questions so that the children really have to think about what is being requested.

Give the children a series of questions which require either multiplication or division operations. Use a wide range of language for the two operations.

What are three fours?

Divide fourteen by two.

Darius has twice as many sweets as Emma. Emma has eight sweets. How many sweets has Darius?

Twenty worms are shared equally between four birds. How many worms do they each have?

Tell the children that they are not required to work out the answers to begin with but must simply write down the sum they will need to do. Go through the results one at a time and discuss what the children have written. On completion, the children can work out the answers.

Give a series of sums with either numbers or symbols missing, for example:

8 ? 2 = 4

☐ × 4 = 20

16 ? 2 = 8

14 ☐ ? = 7

The children must solve the mystery symbol and explain in a sentence how they discovered it.

Give the children some number sentences which show symbols but with some numbers missing, for example, ☐ × △ = 16 or △ ÷ ☐ = 4. Tell the children that the symbols stand for different numbers. Ask them to find the numbers to replace the symbols and make the number sentences true. The children need to know that many different number combinations will work.

Points to watch

Children who do not recognise the required operation or who do not formalise it properly.

Resources

None

Next step

Interpret a wider range of situations involving multiplication or division and explain reasoning.

Making decisions

As the children in Key Stage 1 gradually develop a greater mathematical understanding, they will learn a wider variety of strategies and methods for solving problems. This is right and proper and should be encouraged. Children also have marvellous ways of 'inventing' their own methodologies. Inevitably, then, when coming to solve a problem, they will need to adopt one strategy that is comfortable for them. The critical point for the teacher is whether the strategy works and whether it is the most effective one.

A child should have strategies that work but the teacher's job is to see that not only do they work but they are also effective. As an example, less able children sometimes try to add fairly large numbers by drawing them out as pencil strokes representing each number and then totalling the strokes. If done carefully this strategy does work but is it effective? Children who work with ineffective strategies need to be given other strategies that are better.

A very good way of disseminating strategies is to set problems for the class and have the children explain their methods on the board. Some children will have used the same strategies as others but often an interesting refinement or modification appears which can be discussed. Sometimes children will decide on a strategy which is either not very effective or does not work at all. This needs to be handled in a caring way but the point still has to be made that the strategy needs to be changed. Children are often fascinated by other children's methods and such discussions help to deepen their understanding of mathematics.

Class discussions of strategies can be valuable but time consuming. More and more teachers now ask children to explain in writing how they have tackled a problem. This does not just apply to selecting equipment for a measuring exercise, it also relates to methods of calculating. The process of explanation of method and stating why a strategy has been chosen cannot start early enough and, although infant children may not be able to record justifications for their decisions in writing, they could be written out by an adult or put on tape to be replayed later to the class.

Solve simple puzzles and problems

Learning outcome

To choose and use appropriate number operations and mental strategies to solve problems (Y1)

To choose and use efficient calculation strategies to solve problems (Y2)

Assumed knowledge and experience

The children should have had opportunities to work with the four rules in various ways including written, oral and mental. They should be aware that number problems might be solved using different strategies.

Mathematical importance

It is important to know that different methods exist for solving problems – having a range of strategies can be useful. It is also important to know that some methods are quicker than others.

Activities

Early decision making will be based upon the children thinking for themselves about what they have to do and what equipment they might need to solve a problem. Year 1 children may well need guidance to begin with.

Tell the children that you are going to give them some problems to solve and it will be up to them to choose how they work out the answers. Point out the available resources. Also tell them that they may work out the problems mentally but, if they do, they must write down their method. Give out a series of differentiated activity sheets making sure that the questions are slightly different for each group, this will force them into considering resource options. The least able children could have 8 + 9 + 10, the main group might have 16 × 3 and the most able ones might be given 36 ÷ 9. Allow them time to talk about how they will solve the problem, then give them a few minutes to select apparatus and begin work.

Stop the children after a short while and ask how they are getting on. Do not ask for the answer. Begin to go around each group and find out which resources they have chosen and why.

Allow time for the majority of groups to finish at least a few problems, then sit the children down. Have

each group explain what they had to solve and why they chose the resources they selected. The least able children may find it difficult to articulate their reasoning but they must be encouraged to do so. Discuss points as they arise. Repeat similar exercises every so often so that the children get into the habit of explaining their decisions.

Target particular strategies to see if the children have learnt them and can use them. For example, ask the children to add 9p, 17p and 9p. Have them write down their methods. Did they rearrange the order and put the 17p first? Did they consider doubling the 9p? Did they count on, using a number line or number square? Did they use plastic coins? Did they think about checking the answers by adding the amounts in a different order?

Give each differentiated group a series of number sentences where the operation required is unknown. Each group should have at least one sentence for each operation although the numbers or amounts used with the less able children should be smaller than those for the most able children, sums like 18 × 2 = 36. The children must explain why they opt for a particular operation.

Points to watch

Using a slow or inappropriate method or continuing with the same method when others have been shown to be faster.

Resources

Counters; cubes; 1–100 number square; 1–100 number line; plain paper; squared paper; plastic coins

Next step

Knowing a range of strategies and selecting a preferred method.

Reasoning

Reasoning skills are closely allied to those of making decisions. The ability to reason means deploying strategies in effective ways so that a successful result can be achieved. At such a young age, children have very few mathematical strategies at their disposal but that should not inhibit reasoning. It just means the opportunities will not be so great. Nevertheless, work solving puzzles and examining patterns provide excellent practice in approaching problems sensibly, examining the strategies and methods available, and bringing knowledge to bare in order to gain a good outcome.

Working with patterns is especially important in the infants. The patterns may well be with shapes but teachers should not feel restricted by the coloured 2-D plastic shapes they have at their disposal. Patterns are all around and looking for patterns in the classroom, the school, at home and in the environment can be interesting and provide good material for a pattern display. Make patterns using conkers, pebbles, lunchboxes, fruit, coloured felt-tips, and so on. Bigger-scale patterns can be made in PE or on the playground. Patterns can be seen in words and in pictures.

Patterns and their relationship with numbers are also very appropriate to this age. Mark off every fifth number on a number line and have the children continue the pattern. Look for patterns in the multiples of 2, 5, 10 and some of the other numbers using a 1–100 number square. Tell the children that half the class can play with the sponge balls; ask how many that is. Look for opportunities to set small puzzles all the time.

A most important aspect of reasoning is forming what might be called a hypothesis. From this working theory, the children should be able to predict. Tell the children you have 50p in 5p coins but have to spend 5p on a biscuit every playtime. How many playtimes will it be until you run out of money? What will happen if the cost of a biscuit goes up to 10p?

Through all of this work, the children must be encouraged to tell each other how they are thinking and be given opportunities to display good reasoning.

Explain how problems are solved

Learning outcome

To solve simple mathematical problems or puzzles (Y1 and Y2)

Assumed knowledge and experience

The children should have had experience working with numbers to 100 and some experience with the four rules in written, oral and mental forms. They should know that a symbol can stand for an unknown number.

Mathematical importance

Reasoning is very close to making decisions but actually takes the children on slightly in that it concentrates on putting their chosen method into practice.

Activities

Activities that require the children to find a mystery number have been dealt with elsewhere but a classic problem which children enjoy is of the following type 'I am a number between 0 and 20 what is my name?'. Some children will just want to suggest numbers at random. This is not a good strategy and others should be suggested although the clues will become more sophisticated as the children's knowledge grows. For infants, suggest they ask 'Are you odd or even?', 'Are you a multiple of 10?' or 'Do you have one digit or two?'. To begin with, it is worth recording the children's questions and the results on the board. Later, the children can record the clues they have discovered for themselves.

Function machines can be made very interesting to look at and present number puzzles in an interesting form. Making a 3-D machine is always fun for young children. It must have an In section and an Out section. With either a drawing or model, place a number in the In section, make some machine-type noises and take a number from the Out section. Ask the children how the two numbers are connected. Depending on age, the way in which the Out number has been generated can become more complex. Usually one set of numbers is not enough so give three or four more sets. Above opposite are some sets that could be used with infants.

3 – 7	4 – 8	5 – 9
6 – 10	1 – 2	2 – 4
3 – 6	4 – 8	9 – 5
7 – 3	5 – 1	

Give each child a number. The number itself can be differentiated according to the ability of the child. Have each child write some facts about the number. The facts can involve everyday information or be numerical, for example: 'It is my age', 'It is the number of my house', 'It is the age of the cat', 'I have this number of models', 'This number is the same as 15 add 6', 'It is 19 minus 4', 'It is two lots of three'.

Use plastic coins. Pretend it's a shopping trip and the children have to buy something for a certain amount. Give them the amount and tell them to make that amount using the least number of coins.

Throw two or three dice together and find the totals. How many possible totals are there? Can a total be achieved in different ways? What are the highest and lowest numbers that can be made?

Points to watch

Children who cannot reason a strategy for solving the problem, especially with the function machine.

Resources

A drawn or 3-D function machine; plastic coins; dice

Next step

Using all four operations with larger numbers.

Patterns and relationships

Learning outcome

To recognise and predict from simple patterns and relationships (Y1 and Y2)

Assumed knowledge and experience

The children should know the number names up to at least 10. They should have experience of working with simple shapes and some experience with tracing.

Mathematical importance

Recognition of patterns is a very useful skill that leads on to strategies for searching for more intricate patterns at Key Stage 2.

Activities

Have the children sit and watch as you begin to build a pattern on the board using simple shapes. For this activity, it is best if the children sit at their places or in rows but not in a circle. Magnetic whiteboards and shapes are best for this exercise but if necessary the shapes could be drawn. Draw a circle followed by a square. Now draw another circle and square. Ask all the children to name the shapes out loud as you point to them. Tell them that you want to continue this pattern but are not sure what comes next. Ask them what they think comes next. If they are unsure, return to the drawings and repeat the naming of the shapes. Draw a circle in the next position and ask what will come next. Repeat the activity with two different shapes, then with a three-shape repeat pattern.

Use coloured plastic 2-D shapes. Give the shapes to the children and have them create patterns of their own. They can trace around the shapes and transfer their patterns to A3 paper. Each child must then pass their patterns to someone else who must select the correct 2-D templates and continue the patterns.

Do similar activities but make the patterns slightly less obvious. Start by having two of each shape next to each other, for example, two squares, two circles, two squares, two circles. Move on to a pattern like square, square, circle, square, square, circle. Do not go too far with the complexity but push the children a little.

With the children working in pairs, have one child make a simple rule to do with addition or subtraction, for example, add two to every number. The child writes the rule down on a card which they conceal from their partner. The other child now says a number of their own choice and the child with the card uses the rule to establish another number using their partner's number. This happens three times and after the third time the first child has to explain the rule. Most children should be able to write down the numbers as they develop and so help themselves to solve the mystery rule that is being applied. The children swap roles after each round. This activity can be extended in many ways. The more able children may want to double or halve. Children might like to make a rule such as double and then subtract one. These can be very difficult to solve but may be worth trying with more able Year 2 children.

Use a 1–100 number square (see *Blueprints Maths Key Stage 1: Pupil Resource Book* page 88). Tell the children that you are going to point to a number. Do something to that number, then point to another number. What have you done to the first number? It may be best to operate the mystery rule a number of times and mark each number with felt-tip as you go. Ask the children to predict what the next two numbers will be.

Points to watch

Children who are successful with the shapes activities but unsure with the numbers.

Resources

Coloured 2-D shapes; A3 paper; 1–100 number square

Next step

Solve puzzles and problems in ever widening contexts, particularly with number.

Explain in writing and orally

Learning outcome

To explain how a problem was solved either verbally, through a scribe or by writing (Y2)

Assumed knowledge and experience

The children should know a variety of strategies for dealing with numbers and be confident enough with numbers to recognise how number knowledge and strategies may be adapted to solve different types of problems.

Mathematical importance

Children should be able to talk through their thinking processes. This is an important skill which helps the child to think with clarity and also helps the teacher find out what is going wrong – if anything.

Activities

These activities are similar to some earlier activities but the emphasis here must be on the clarity of the explanations being offered.

Ask the children to add the numbers in adjacent pairs; for example, 1 and 2, 2 and 3, 3 and 4, and so on. More able children should be able to begin from larger numbers. Have them record the totals using the + and = symbols. Ask the children if they notice anything about the numbers being produced as totals (always odd numbers). Can they explain why this might be?

Tell the children that you have made the number 14 by adding three smaller numbers. The three numbers are different and all are multiples of 2. How many number combinations can they find that fit the rules? Children must explain to the rest of the class how they worked them out. Repeat this with a different number and different sets of rules, for example, all odd numbers.

Write five different coin amounts on the board, for example, 1p, 5p, 10p, 20p, and 50p. The children

have to total the amounts to find the highest amount they can using two, three or four coins, depending upon ability. What is the largest total they can achieve? The task is fairly straightforward but insist that they clearly explain the reasoning for the answer they give.

Strictly following safety rules for the school, take the children to the car park and have them write down the car numbers. Back in class, have them total the digits to begin with, then, if the total is more than nine, total the digits again to give a single figure, for example, with X476JAG, add 4, 7 and 6 which makes 17, then add the 1 and 7 to make 8. This task is interesting and fairly straightforward. Now ask them to do the same thing with any three-digit numbers and find which combinations give the highest total. Give 678 as an example, these add to 21 and then 3. Point out that a lower number, like 112, actually totals more: 4! So what combination can they come up with that reaches 9? How did they work it out?

Points to watch

Children who successfully work on a problem but are not capable of explaining their reasoning – the lesson objective! Children who simply cannot find a suitable strategy.

Resources

Plastic coins

Next step

Problem solving exercises and situations that need the use of more than one operation and with larger numbers or amounts.

Problems

In order for children to really learn mathematics, they need to know that the subject has some value and might even be fun! In 'real life' we do not often need to solve many mathematical problems and in general an estimated answer will do – do I have enough money this month to buy petrol and food! Nevertheless, being able to work calculations when needed can be very useful and all children have the right to such knowledge.

Problem solving might often be thought of as a calculation disguised by words. The skill of problem solving is in sorting out the various elements that need to be dealt with: what operation is needed and what numbers are involved? For example, a child has 23 teeth but four fall out; how many teeth are left? The problem is twofold: what calculation strategy needs to be used to resolve the problem and what are the numbers involved. In this case, the child is likely to use a subtraction method and work with the numbers 23 and 4. The sum should appear as 23 – 4 and may be done on paper, using equipment, or mentally.

Interestingly, if the problem had been, a child has 23 teeth but 17 fall out, how many teeth are left, the child may well consider an adding-on strategy to be more suitable and count on from 17 to 23. This tells us that very many problem-solving activities can be approached using different strategies. In general, it is very good for children to learn more than one strategy. The more 'weapons' they have at their disposal, the more likely they are to find one which is suitable for a particular set of circumstances.

Although a range of strategies should be encouraged, great care needs to be taken with the less able children who may struggle to hold one method in mind so that more than one confuses them. Of course, you will use different ways of teaching and explaining. The hope is always that every child will end up with various strategies but sometimes reality sets in and if a child is secure with one strategy that may be satisfactory.

Solving 'real life' problems

Learning outcome

To solve 'real life' problems using methods already learnt (Y1 and Y2)

Assumed knowledge and experience

The children should have worked with numbers to at least 20 and 100 in Year 2. They should know some strategies for solving simple problems and be able to make decisions about which are the most effective methods. They should have some knowledge of the monetary system would also be an advantage.

Mathematical importance

Most of the mathematics that we encounter arises out of 'real life' problems. These problems are usually trivial in nature to the young child but they do need to realise that mathematics is a living subject and not simply an excuse for teachers to give lots of sums.

Activities

The main difference between these activities and some others that require numbers to be manipulated is that they will usually appear in a word context. This means that the children will need to pick up the clues about the operation that is needed and sort the clues from the rest of the information.

Give the children a series of questions that are as 'real life' as possible, for example:

Pedro and Rio have sixteen chicken nuggets to share between them. How many do they each have?

Sabrina's birthday is on the twenty-third. Today is the eleventh. How many days until her birthday?

Taj has to collect 50 cards but so far he only has eighteen. How many more does he need?

A netball team scores sixteen goals. The other team scores twice as many. How many is that?

Maria needs 85p for a chocolate bar. She has 64p. How much more does she need?

Once this has been done with the whole class, have each child invent some 'real life' problems of their own. This may be done in writing or, more likely, through speech. Some children might like to record their questions on a tape for the whole class to try.

You may want to record some of the best questions for use with another class or next year. The only rules are that the answers must be whole numbers or amounts – no fractions – and the person setting the question must also work out the answer so that it can be checked. You act as umpire!

Use a list or partial list of football results. Local matches would be most interesting but otherwise use Premier League games. Photocopy the list and give it to the children. Ask questions based on the scores: 'Which team or teams scored the most goals?', 'Who scored the least?', 'Which match produced the most goals?', 'What was the total score for all the games?'

Write a 'secret' number on a piece of card. Use 23 as an example. Tell the children that the number is between 0 and 30 and they must guess what it is and write their guess on a piece of paper. Reveal the secret number and ask a few questions; for example, 'Whose number was closest?', 'Whose was farthest away?'. How far was each child from the secret number and which guesses were more than two/five/ten out?

Points to watch

Failure to sort out an effective strategy.

Resources

Football league tables

Next step

Problems with larger numbers and sums of money involved. Problems with time and measures.

Money

Working with money is an early means through which children may be shown that mathematics is strongly connected to skills we need for life. This work also helps generally to reinforce the learning that is taking place with number. Children will be learning about the growth of number from 10 to 20 or 30 and then on to 100 and beyond. At around the same time, the coins to 20p will be introduced and gradually extended to £1, £2 and then the notes. This connection between numbers in the abstract and numbers related to coins can be hard for some children to see. Ask a young child in Year 1 to add five and three and they will probably say eight, but ask the same child to add 5p and 3p and they may well be stumped. The step can be difficult for some children and really asks the question: have they really grasped the meaning of number? This difficulty reveals itself again when work on measurement begins with centimetres and metres.

It should not be assumed that children necessarily have much understanding about money or coins at the infant stage. They may well have plenty of things and even be given pocket money but that is different to understanding the relationship between the coins and their values. This understanding needs to be built up in a logical way at school. As with the number system, the children need opportunities to get used to what the coins look like and come to learn their

names. They will see similarities between the coins but also differences. They must learn to recognise the coins instantly. Once the coin names are learnt, the next step is to indicate that they are not continuous as with the number system. The coins are not valued 1p, 2p, 3p, 4p, 5p, and so on. It is important to ask 'why not?'. Then it is time to look at how we can make up the 'missing' coins by combining the ones we do have. Eventually, the children will come to add the coins in various ways, use them to make simple purchases, work out total costs and pay with exact amounts. They will also work out how to give change.

As with most other number work at this age, it is important that children see work with money as being real. The use of a class 'shop' or producing shopping lists may not be very original but they are still very meaningful to infants. Unfortunately, children nowadays cannot buy many items for the small sums we deal with at the early stages of monetary work; nevertheless, the practical grounding in 'real life' situations is necessary. Plastic coins are very useful and the more realistic the better. Facsimile coins can now be bought which are magnetic and the correct size in proportion to each other. Coin fans are available. The widest range of resources should be used.

Recognise coins of different values

Learning outcome

To recognise coins of different values (Y1)

To recognise all coins and begin to use £/p notation (Y2)

Assumed knowledge and experience

Children will have a general knowledge about money and the coins we use through everyday life experiences. Some very young children are given money to spend and may well be acquainted with all the coins and notes. Children are likely to be familiar with handling coins.

Mathematical importance

It is important for children to realise that 100 of one unit can be converted into 1 of another unit. The same will apply with centimetres and metres.

Activities

Talk to the children about the money they know and use. Write on the board the coin values and encourage them to describe what the coins look like. Give out a selection of 1p, 2p, 5p and 10p coins to each table and ask the children just to look at them at first. After a few minutes, have the children tell you what they have noticed: the colours are different, the sizes are different. Finally, have the children sort the coins in different ways. This sorting activity neatly fits into work on handling data. Encourage the children to relate the sorting exercises to the names of the coins and use the correct terminology; for example, the 1p and 2p are both brown, the 1p is smaller than the 2p, the 2p and 10p are different colours.

Set up a home corner where the children can 'buy' items which have been labelled with prices in the range 1–10p. Note that these prices should exactly match coin values and not require a combination of coins being tendered – that comes later! In small groups, have some children act as shopkeepers with others as customers.

When some familiarity has grown with the 1–10p coins, introduce the 20p and 50p. Compare these two with the others already learnt. Have each child or group of children, arrange the coins in a row according to face values. Leave a gap between each coin. Call out the name of a coin and the children must slap their hands over the coin to cover it as quickly as possible. The children can play the same game in pairs. Introduce the £1 and £2 coins.

Notation (Y2). Give out plastic coins up to the value of 50p. Ask the children to make a collection of coins to the value of 99p. The less able children may work in groups but the main group and the more able children should work individually. The children can use as few or as many coins as they like. Give them a few minutes to reach the total. Ask them what will happen if they add 1p to this. How much will they have? Tell them that 100p is the same as £1. Show them a real pound coin and ask if they have seen one before. Ask what colour it is. Is it a different colour from the other colours? Ask them why. What is special about it? It is the same as 100p but we do not want to keep writing 100p so we write £1.00 instead. Tell them that the dot separates the pounds from the pennies; what is on the left of it shows the pounds and what is on the right of it shows the pennies.

Write £1.30 on the board. Tell them it says one pound and 30 pence. Now write other amounts on the board, such as £0.56, £0.28, £0.45, £1.56, £1.80, and have the children say the amounts. Tell them that if they only have pennies, they write 0 on the left of the dot. Give examples such as 10p which is written as £0.10 which means no pounds and ten pennies. Write plenty of examples on the board and have the children give the names of the amounts. Be sure to tell them that we do not write the £ sign and the p sign in the same amount. We only use one of the signs and it is almost always the £ sign.

Points to watch

Not recognising the significance of the dot as a separator of pounds and pennies.

Resources

Plastic coins

Next step

The value of all coins and translating between amounts such as 157p and £1.57.

Find total, give change/Choose which coins

Learning outcome

To find totals and change from up to 20p (Y1)

To find totals, give change and work out which coins to pay with (Y2)

Assumed knowledge and experience

The children should be able to recognise the coins and their values up to 20p and be able to add numbers together to at least 10. In general, they should have opportunities to use plastic coins in play situations such as play shops. It is very likely that they have had some experience with handling real coins and spending them with adult guidance. Some will receive weekly pocket money.

Mathematical importance

This work gives valuable support to reinforcing addition and subtraction in situations that have some reality. Do not underestimate the fact that, although children may be able to add, for example, 8 and 1, adding 8p and 1p may seem completely different.

Activities

Begin by reminding the children of the coins we use up to the value of 20p. Show them real coins if possible or use pictures, magnetic representations or coin fans. Ask them what they would do if they had to buy something for 3p. Bring out the point that 3p can be made in different ways; ask them how many different ways. How about 4p, how many ways could that be made? Continue on the same theme to a reasonable level depending upon ability. The more able children will begin to make lots of ways for 20p or more, so ask them to make the amount with as few coins as possible.

This activity is similar to the one above. Have the children choose three different coins. They must total this amount and write it down. Now they must make up the same amount by using different coins. The activity may be repeated using different numbers of coins.

Use Activity sheet 62 which shows various items with their costs. Have the children begin by making a simple shopping list based on the items shown. They may cut out the items and stick them on to another piece of paper rather than try to write out the words. Once they have established their own list, they may use

plastic coins if necessary to total the price of their list. Another child should check the list total. The children may need to be given some direction about how much they have to spend and the less able ones may need guidance on how many items they can buy.

Using the same basic activity, have one child act as the 'shopkeeper' and another as the 'customer'. When the items are presented for payment, each child must total their list and see if they agree. The customer must then always buy with the single coin which represents the amount due or a bit more; for example, if the total is 17p, a 20p coin should be offered. The shopkeeper then has to work out the change and the customer must agree.

Do not use plastic coins and insist on the answers using correct notation with the p sign. Set a target amount such as 12p and write it on the board. Now ask various questions to test the children's knowledge. Ask questions such as: 'I paid with a 10p and a 5p. How much change should I receive?', 'I paid using three coins. Which ones?', 'I have 10p. How much more do I need?' Repeat this with different target amounts.

Points to watch

Children who only feel safe using 1p coins when making larger amounts.

Resources

Plastic coins; coin fans

Next step

Find exact amounts up to at least 20p.

Paying exact sums using small coins

Learning outcome

To work out how to pay an exact sum using smaller coins (Y1)

Assumed knowledge and experience

The children should have had experience working with numbers to at least 20, including reading and knowing the number names. They should have had play experiences with coins and know the shapes and values of coins to at least 20p. They should also have had some experience with number sentences and with the = sign.

Mathematical importance

This work reinforces addition and subtraction in the context of money.

Activities

Allow the children a few minutes to play with the coins and then remind them of the values they should know. Have the children place in order one of each coin up to the value of 20p. Put the other coins out of the way. Tell them that they are going to make up different amounts just using these coins. You will also want them to write the amounts. Now have each of them put a 2p and a 1p together. Ask what amount they have in total. Have the children write down this amount as a number sentence, for example, 2p + 1p = 3p. Individual whiteboards are useful to ensure a quick and correct response from each child.

Now have them repeat the exercise with a 5p and a 1p. Continue the activity with the children making as many different amounts as they can but only using the particular coins they have in front of them, two at a time. The main group and more able children can move on to three or more of the coins in combination.

As a continuation of the activity, prepare a sheet that goes from 1p to 38p. The children must write a sum for each amount that gives the total but only using combinations of single coins, as shown opposite for example.

Coins	Amount
1p	1p
2p	2p
1p + 2p	3p
	4p
5p	5p
5p + 1p	6p
5p + 2p	7p
5p + 2p + 1p	8p
	9p
10p	10p

Once the list is complete, some amounts will not be represented. Have the children work out the minimum number of coins that could go together to make up each of those amounts.

Use Activity sheet 64 which shows a selection of items and their cost. Each item is accompanied by a number of boxes that represent the minimum number of coins needed to make that amount. The children must work in pairs and complete the boxes. Discuss this with the children and have them make up their own amounts to give as a test to their partner.

Points to watch

Incorrect additions and poor writing of the p sign.

Resources

Plastic coins

Next step

Solving simple money word problems.

Translate between pounds and pennies

Learning outcome

To translate between pounds and pennies, for example, £1.07 is 107p (Y2)

Assumed knowledge and experience

The children should know that 100 pennies are equivalent to £1. They should be familiar with all the coins to £2 and with using the coins to make up amounts, find totals and give change.

Mathematical importance

The children need to know that working with monetary values is a very important application of mathematics in the real world.

Activities

Remind the children that 100 pennies are equivalent to £1 and how we write one pound as £1.00 (see page 72). Have the children count on from 100, first just as numbers, then including p for pennies. They only need to go to about 120. Write some of the amounts on the board, for example, 107p, 115p and 120p. Say again that 100p is £1 and we can write 115p as £1.15. The dot separates the whole pounds from the pennies. Repeat this with 120p. Now ask them to represent 107p on individual whiteboards or on paper. Do a quick check to see how they have written the amount. It is likely that some will have written £1.7 or £1.70. It is critical that this error is picked up early. Tell the children that there are always two numbers after the dot to represent the pennies and that if there is less than 10p beyond the pound, we must write a 0 before the number of pennies. Ask how 101p would be written. Move on to amounts such as 150p, 180p. Make sure they are not being confused with £1.05 and £1.08, respectively. Write different amounts with signs and numbers and then as words, have the children say the words out loud and compare the amounts in pennies with those in pounds and pennies.

With the children working in pairs with plastic coins, including the £2, have one child make up amounts that the other child has to write down in figures and with the correct notation. Tell the children to try and trick their friends by making amounts such as £3.09.

Although we normally tell children to write money in the form £2.56, for example, it is correct to write 256p but this form is not often seen. It is incorrect to use both signs, for example, £2.56p. This must be pointed out.

This activity reinforces all of those above but may be most suitable for the main and more able group. Write a series of amounts on the board in the normal notation, for example, £1.03, £2.05, £3.07, £4.03, £5.30, £2.90. Have the children reduce each amount by a sum that will frequently, but not always, mean crossing the pound/pennies boundary; for example, by 12p. In most of the above cases, this will test the children's understanding of amounts such as £1.03 and whether they can subtract across the pound/pennies boundary.

Use Activity sheet 65 which shows groups of the same amount in three ways: pennies, pounds and pennies, and in words. The three ways are jumbled and the children must match the representations.

Points to watch

Incorrect writing of the penny values from 1 to 9. Misuse or non-use of the £ and p signs.

Next step

Introduction and use of the notes.

Resources

Plastic coins including £2; individual whiteboards

Handling data

Dealing with information in a mathematical way can offer plenty of opportunities for exciting work. It also helps to reinforce and strengthen links with other subjects, notably ICT. Some of the basics of handling data such as lists can seem a bit simple, even for Year 1 children, but it is most important that the children have plenty of activities to deepen their understanding and lots of opportunities to hear the correct vocabulary being used in context.

Early work with handling information often begins with sorting exercises. Young children are used to sorting, very often with toys, and so the leap to sorting by colour or shape is not too far. What does differ between home-based activities and those in the classroom is the need to then represent the results of the sorting in some form of array. The range of infant displays of information is fairly small but still important, as they form the basis for what will come later. The displays must be clear and easy to read. They should represent accurate information and be well labelled and enable questions to be answered.

In the past, children have not always been successful at handling data because they have often been required just to place data in various formats. The purpose of data is to answer questions and so the emphasis in the National Numeracy Strategy and through all good textbooks is on good presentation but even more on interrogating the data. Children must get into the habit of asking themselves if the information is clear, whether a better representational method could be chosen and if the problem can be solved through this medium.

Handling data should be looked on as a two-way process. From one end, the children should be given or develop a problem. They then find appropriate information and sort it. Finally, they put the information into a format which enables the problem to be solved. From the other end, children should be able to look at information already prepared by way of lists, tables, graphs, and directly answer questions. They need plenty of both types of experiences.

Sort objects – lists and tables

Learning outcome

To solve a problem by sorting, classifying and organising information in simple ways – lists and tables (Y1)

Assumed knowledge and experience

The children will be using and learning the numbers and number names to 20 and beyond. They will be starting to think in terms of combining groups of numbers to make a total and, possibly, organising numbers as odds and evens.

Mathematical importance

Not all mathematical problems consist of sums. Some problems rely on sorting information and organising it in ways that will be useful. From the organised information, deductions can be made as well as predictions.

Activities

Write the numbers 1 to 9 on the board but jumbled up and with the number 7 missing, for example, 8 2 4 9 1 5 3 6. Tell the children that they are going to list the numbers in order starting from 1 and that they will need to sort them out. Explain that listing means making a group in a special order. Also say that you have deliberately left one number out, so as they list, they must look for the missing number. Have a child tell you which number should go first in this list. Have a number track near and visible if necessary. Write the 1 and continue.

Throughout this simple exercise, keep repeating something like 'What number needs to be written next in the list?'. After 6, ask what comes next and when 7 is proffered, ask if it is there. Tell them that sorting the numbers into order and listing them has helped to solve the problem of the missing number.

This activity may be extended in all sorts of ways as the children's knowledge of number grows. With older children, similar exercises may be carried out with odd and even numbers, multiples of 5 or 10, months of the year, and so on. The important teaching point is that a solution is possible because of a logical sorting and listing process.

Who has the longest first name? Have the children on each table sort out their names so that they can find out whose name has the least number of letters and whose has the most. Compare the results of one table with those of another and discuss them.

How much fruit? Choose a selection of children who have packed lunches. During the course of a week, collect information of how many pieces of fruit each child has. You may want to count grapes separately! In the following week, make a table of the children's names and the numbers of pieces of fruit. Ask the children questions relating to the list, for example, 'Who had the most pieces?', 'Who had more than Jamie?', 'Who had three bananas?'.

Which month has the most birthdays? Tell the children that this is the problem they must solve. Have the children consider how they could find out how many children were born in each month. Discuss methods of finding the information to begin with. Next go on to how the information can be organised and together work out a table format. Collect and sort the information as a class, then answer the question.

Points to watch

Children who cannot see methods of sorting, especially if number knowledge is weak.

Resources

Registers

Next step

Representing information with pictures and pictograms.

Sort and classify – pictures/pictograms

Learning outcome

To solve a problem by collecting, sorting and organising information using pictures (Y1) and pictograms (Y2)

Assumed knowledge and experience

The children should be familiar with terms such as collecting and sorting – probably from earlier work on lists and tables (see page 77). They should have worked with numbers to at least 20 (Y1) and 100 (Y2).

Mathematical importance

Collecting good-quality information and making deductions and predictions from it is a very useful tool in many walks of life. Clear presentation of information is also a very valuable skill.

Activities

The activity needs to go through a process that is clear and can be repeated whatever the particular problem. This activity will centre on finding out about favourite kinds of children's television programmes. Tell the children that they are going to find out which programmes they prefer. Ask them how this could be discovered. Lead them to suggest categories and voting. Young children can find categorisation a bit difficult so they are likely to need some prompting. Once the voting has taken place, the work needs to move on to showing the information in a helpful way.

For this activity, the children should come up with a symbol to represent the category, for example, a mouse for cartoons, football for sports. The symbols must be agreed upon and then drawn. Each child can draw the symbol for their favourite type of programme. Discuss how the information can be shown and produce a finished information picture. Label the picture.

Complete the activity by asking questions about the information the children have found. Other themes could be favourite food, drinks and sports. The more able children can work out the total of how many children were asked and how many were in each category. Being asked if the information would be the same if three-year-olds or twelve-year-olds had been asked should extend all the children. Ask them why it might be different.

Pictograms are an excellent way of showing information, especially with children whose reading and writing is limited. Say to the class that you want to find out about their favourite foods. Agree on some categories, for example, roast, Chinese, Indian, fish and chips, salads. A quick show of hands will provide the information. It can be worthwhile at this stage to have a catch-all category of 'other'. Discuss how the information can be shown and lead them to the idea of a symbol being used to represent one child. Tell them that information shown using symbols is called a pictogram. Decide on a suitable symbol. The usual smiley face is okay but children will enjoy the activity more if something inventive is found, perhaps a simple facial expression representing hunger could be agreed upon and used by the children when they draw their own pictogram representing this information. On completion of the information array, make sure questions are asked or, better still, have the children invent questions.

After a few similar activities, challenge the children with some intriguing questions and statements; for example, 'I think you all believe Friday is the best day of the week!' or 'When I was a child I had 20p pocket money a week; I bet you get more'. Split the class into groups and see if they can go through the process of establishing the problem to be solved, working out how to gather information, displaying it and then answering the question. Be careful when they all want to ask everyone else questions at the same time – some structure is needed!

Points to watch

Poor categorisation leading to large numbers of sections.

Resources

Computer programs; drawing tools

Next step

Pictograms where symbols may represent more than one object.

Sort and classify – lists

Learning outcome

To solve problems through compiling lists and tables and interrogating the information (Y2)

Assumed knowledge and experience

The children should have worked with simple lists and tables in Year 1. They should understand that information can be collected, sorted, displayed and used in a variety of ways that enable questions to be asked and answered. They should have knowledge of the number system, including multiples of 2, 5 and 10.

Mathematical importance

Children must realise that different methods of organising information exist and that the clarity of the data array is very important in finding answers and solutions to problems.

Activities

Remind the children of the meaning of list and listing. Give a series of small differentiated activities to each ability group. The children will simply be required to solve a problem aligned with the activity; for example:

List the odd numbers from 12 to 30. Which ones are also multiples of 5?

List the numbers from 50 to 65. Which numbers are odd?

List the letters of the alphabet from A to T. Which letters are vowels?

List the coins from 1p to £1. Which coins are silver?

Show the children Activity sheet 68. Ask the children questions about the information on the activity sheet that deliberately include and introduce particular vocabulary. Highlight the vocabulary as you go. Ask questions such as, 'What does the information show?', 'Do the labels help you?', 'Which is the most popular?' and 'What does this information represent?'. Write up or printout the specialist vocabulary and make it part of a display.

Have the children work in groups. Each group will produce a table and questions to go with it that will become the main display. Children will probably find it difficult to find a 'problem' to solve or situation

they would like to research. The following suggestions should be successful with most children.

Have a group of less able children collect and sort information about favourite seasons. After collecting the data, they must decide on how to present it. Finally, they must write some questions for the rest of the class to answer.

The main group could investigate the most common vowel using books. They may need guidance on the means for collecting the information, especially guidance on how many words to examine! The data array should be straightforward but they should be challenged to ask interesting questions, for example: 'Would the result be the same for books of a different age range?', 'Would books in another language give the same result?' This group could also investigate favourite colours, cars, actors, football teams.

The more able group could be asked to investigate the most common word length. It is best to limit this activity to words of up to six letters. The group needs to question how many words they should investigate, what is a fair sample, what type of book they should use, and whether fiction and non-fiction would give different results.

Points to watch

Poor or simple repetitive questions. Poor use or non-use of mathematical vocabulary.

Resources

Fiction and non-fiction books

Next step

Using frequency tables.

Simple block graphs

Learning outcome

To solve a problem through collecting information and presenting it as a block graph (Y2)

Assumed knowledge and experience

The children should have had experience with collecting, sorting and displaying data in order to answer questions. This earlier work is likely to have been with simple lists, tables and pictograms. They should have devised questions based on information arrays.

Mathematical importance

This is another form of pictorial representation that clearly shows information and allows interrogation in order to answer questions.

Activities

Ask the children to decide on their favourite chocolate bar out of a list you give them. Give five of the most common brands and tell them they must select one. Draw a horizontal line on the board and label it with the names of the brands. Leave a gap between the names. Go through the brands one by one and as each child names their favourite, just put a squiggle in the column above the name. Leave gaps between the columns as you go. When this is complete, tell the children that they are now going to look at a better way of showing the information and it is called a block graph. Tell the children that you are going to put one square in each column instead of each squiggle. Have the children count the squiggles, rub them out and draw a column of the correct number of squares. Repeat this across the array. On completion, have the children suggest labels for each axis and an overall title. Write these on the board. Explain that a block graph is a very neat way of showing information. Ask some questions about the block graph.

This next activity involves the children finding information in order to test a hypothesis. The children should test the statement 'blue is the most popular colour'. Ask the children how they could gather this information. They will probably say by asking other children but suggest they may investigate colours on such things as cars. This may be appropriate for the more able children. If an

assistant is available, have at least one group research the colours of cars in the car park or going past the school. Stick with the main colours, rather than all the shades and metallic varieties. Allow a suitable period for the observation; a busy road will generate enough information in 5 minutes, a country lane may take all day! The rest of the class can ask friends. Have each group present the information as a drawn version and as a 3-D version by using connecting cubes. Both versions should be properly labelled and have titles. The children must also devise questions to go with the block graphs. Challenge the more able ones to think of other ways they could test the hypothesis, for example, paints used on walls, casual clothing worn by children or carpets at home. Some children might also like to find out if one colour has always been the favourite, whether it depend upon the season, fashion or country. This is an ideal opportunity to use the Internet to contact schools abroad for information.

Show the children Activity sheet 69 which shows data arranged as a block graph. The example has labelled axes but not a title. Have the children suggest possible titles. Have each child come up with at least one question that could be answered by looking at the block graph. Give the children an extra piece of information that needs to be shown on the same block graph. Have a few up to the board to show where it should go and how it should be labelled.

Points to watch

Children who are producing a finished block graph but fail to see it as a means of showing data.

Resources

Cubes

Next step

Using bar charts.

Measures

Most children tend to have a vague notion of time, distance, weight and capacity but little real understanding of any of the meanings to do with their measurement. Children will often use words and expressions like 'really heavy', 'a very long way', 'takes for ages' and 'nearly full' to indicate some form of rudimentary measure. In fact, these expressions are a very good place to start the more formal side of measuring because they represent forms of estimations. Estimating lengths, capacities, weights and amounts of time is a good way into more accurate measurement. Most children will accept quite readily that it is not good enough to say 'the train to Gran's house leaves some time soon' and that it is important to find out exactly when. This being the case, formal work with measuring can usually start with estimating. Once this has been started, it is important to start teaching the standard units that we employ for the type of item being measured. Children will have heard many of these words and phrases being used at home and at school but will have little understanding of their meaning.

Once good-quality estimating has established the need for exactitude, begin with small exercises that focus on the few measures suggested in the National Numeracy Strategy. These measures are fairly easy for children to come to terms with but, like many artificial constructs, require lots of practice to reinforce. It needs to be recognised that the larger the unit, the less quickly children will become used to it. Centimetres usually quickly become second nature, the kilometre may never!

Of all the measuring skills that children come across during the primary years, telling the time and talking about time are often considered the most important, especially by parents! It is often the vocabulary of telling the time that causes children headaches. What exactly does 'quarter to' mean? Children need to have these things explained carefully and often. The presentation of a circular clock is also a novel idea for children who tend to think of numbers as being on a straight line – a number line. The cyclic nature of the clock also causes some confusion. Do not be afraid to teach the main positions with a clock that just has one hand. Once these positions are established, both hands must be shown and used correctly. Constantly relate the idea that 'half past' means 30 minutes past, and so on.

This work should always relate back to the usefulness of accurate measuring. As the work progresses keep returning to 'Why is this useful?' and 'Who might want to know this?'.

Estimate, measure, compare size

Learning outcome

To compare more than two lengths, masses or capacities and begin to use standard units (Y1)

Assumed knowledge and experience

The children will probably have had very little formal experience of comparing amounts. They may well have taken part in cooking activities at home or at pre-school which have involved measuring with mass and capacity but are unlikely to know the units used in any real sense.

Mathematical importance

This introductory work will give basic measuring concepts and skills that can be built upon later. It introduces important vocabulary.

Activities

The children will compare lengths by direct comparison and begin to use some relevant vocabulary. This work will lead to a permanent word bank being built of 'measure' words. Tell the children they are going to compare heights. Stand alongside a member of the class. Say that you are taller than the child. Say that the child is shorter than you. Write 'taller' and 'shorter' on the board. Ask the first five children on the register to stand next to each other. Have the rest of the class make up a sentence using taller and shorter which describes a situation they can see with their friends, for example, 'Ali is taller than Saffron'.

Give out connecting cubes to each table. Tell the children they have 1 minute to make the longest stick they can. At the end of the minute, have the children on each table lay their sticks alongside each other making sure the left ends are all flush. Draw a long narrow rectangle on the board above a short narrow rectangle. Tell the children that we say the top one is longer than the bottom one and that the bottom one is shorter than the top one. Write 'longer' and 'shorter' on the board. Now have the children compare their sticks. Tell them you want to hear the correct words being used. Use cards which say 'is longer than' or 'is shorter than'. Distribute them to each table. Have the children make up comparing 'sentences' using the sticks they have made and the two phrases, for example, _____ is longer than _____ and _____ is shorter than _____.

Do similar activities to include 'high', 'low', 'wide', 'narrow', 'deep', 'shallow', 'thick', 'thin', 'far' and 'near'. Examples can go towards a display.

Bring a full box of A4 photocopier paper into the room and drop it heavily on a table. Ask the children if they think it is heavy. Have a few children try to lift the box – do not let them strain themselves! Now blow a few feathers around. Ask the children if these are heavy. Write 'heavy' and 'light' on the board. Tell the children we can say the box is heavy but the feathers are light. Say that it is not always that easy to compare weights and show them a pencil and a felt-tip. Ask how they could find out which was heavier and which was lighter. Have some balances available. Place the pencil and felt-tip each side of the balance and see what happens. Make some cards which show 'is heavier than' or 'is lighter than'. Give the cards out and either by common sense or through using the balances have the children make up weight 'sentences' on their tables. Some examples can go towards a class display.

Compare capacities by using a standard receptacle, such as an eggcup, then see how many eggcups are equal to various other containers. The children could record the results using tally marks. Introduce 'holds', 'empty' and 'full'.

Points to watch

Children confusing the comparative terms, for example, long and short.

Resources

Linking cubes; A4 photocopier paper; feathers

Next step

Beginning to use the standard units rather than comparisons.

Estimate, measure, compare size/capacity

Learning outcome

To estimate, measure and compare lengths using standard units (Y1)

To estimate, measure and compare mass/capacities using standard units (Y1)

Assumed knowledge and experience

The children will have compared heights and lengths. (see page 82) but not against a standard measure or unit. They should be aware of some of the vocabulary associated with measuring length, mass and capacity.

Mathematical importance

The children need to be introduced to the idea that we need common measurements across the world so that we can discuss lengths, weights and capacities using the same language.

Activities

Take the children into the hall. Have them sit down in the centre of the floor and look at the shortest side. Ask them how many footsteps they think it would take to get from one side to the other. After a minute of thinking, ask them for their estimate. Write the estimate down for each child. Some children will be limited in their knowledge of larger numbers so this is a good excuse to use numbers beyond 20 in a realistic way. Have one child walk across the hall and count out loud as they go. Count with the child if necessary. Does their estimate match the measurement? Let the children walk across the hall in groups of five or ten. Record their results. Go back to the class. Discuss how close each child was to their estimate. Show on the board the range of footsteps that were taken. Now have them estimate other distances, like the longer side of the hall, the playground, the corridor, and see if they can now make a better estimate.

Tell the children that they are going to measure the width of their tables with a standard unit that will be their hand span. Define what a hand span means – the distance between the thumb and little finger when the hand is stretched. Let them estimate the number of hand spans and write it down. Now let them find how many hand spans are equivalent to the desk width. Be prepared to allow parts of hands counting as whole ones! Discuss the comparison of

estimates with the actual results and then do the same thing with width.

Tell the children they are going to use pencils as a standard unit to weigh with. Have the children select three objects they want to weigh. Begin with the children estimating how many pencils will weigh the same as each object. Using the balance, they must place an object on one side and pencils on the other side so they approximately balance, adding or removing pencils until a balance is achieved. Compare estimates with the measurements.

Have a variety of containers ranging from an eggcup to a 2-litre squash bottle. The children work in groups. Give each group the same standard unit such as a cup or Petri dish. Now have each group work out how many standard units are equivalent to the other containers. They should estimate the amounts each time. Some containers may be less than the standard unit, in which case help the children to record 'less than one'. Have each group explain what they did and their results, especially how well their estimates compared with the measurements.

Throughout the above activities, ask the children if the standard unit they are using is good or can they think of a better one. The more able children can try other standard units when practicable.

Points to watch

Children losing count with higher numbers. Estimates not improving.

Next step

Begin to use centimetres, metres, kilograms, grams, litres and millilitres.

Resources

Pencils for weighing; balances; variety of containers

Read simple scales to nearest division

Learning outcome

To read a simple scale to the nearest labelled division (Y2)

Assumed knowledge and experience

The children are likely to have only limited experience of reading scales. They may have used scales in cooking or stood on weighing scales. Although not a scale in the sense of a weighing instrument, children of this age should be used to a number line.

Mathematical importance

Reading scales accurately provides important information in 'real life' situations as well as other subject disciplines such as science and geography.

Activities

Make available to the class a variety of instruments with scales. The more the better.

Put at least one instrument on each table. Tell the children to be careful with them but give them a few minutes to play with the instruments. Move the children to each table in turn. When they have completed the tour, ask what the instruments have in common. Conclude that they all measure something and briefly discuss what they weigh and how they show amounts. Tell the children each one, except the digital scales, has a scale divided into sections. Draw a simple semicircular marked scale on the board with an arrow from the centre pointing to 0 on the left. Mark the scale at five roughly equal intervals and label them 0–5. Tell the children that this is like the scale on many weighing machines and that, for this work, each unit is 1 kg. Ask them what will happen if something heavy is put on the scales; one of the scales can be used to demonstrate. Tell them that the heavier something is, the further the arrow moves. On the same scale, draw the arrow pointing to 2. Ask how much this indicates. Repeat with the other divisions and include some weights that are halfway between. Repeat with a scale that goes to 10.

Give each child a 30 cm ruler and a metre ruler to each table. With the children sitting near you, show them the markings on a metre ruler. These vary according to the maker but the important point to illustrate is how the centimetre and 10 cm divisions are shown. Draw a section of the ruler on the board and have children identify the divisions. To begin with, label the divisions from 0 to 30 in tens. Move on to labelling from 40 to 80 or 60 to 100. Ask the children to measure things in the room but only to the nearest ten (see page 29). Let them choose various objects. The less able children may need to be told which objects to measure. Do a similar activity with a 30 cm ruler, the children measuring to the nearest centimetre.

Points to watch

Children not reading scales to the correct nearest division.

Resources

Variety of instruments with scales, including weighing scales and newton measures

Next step

Reading scales with millimetres and grams. Accurate use of a ruler to measure and draw.

Measure/draw to the nearest centimetre

Learning outcome

To use a ruler to measure and draw lines to the nearest centimetre (Y2)

Assumed knowledge and experience

The children should have worked with various types of scales in order to begin reading them accurately to the nearest division. This work should have included weighing instruments and metre rulers. In general, children will have used rulers for drawing straight lines.

Mathematical importance

Accurate representation of distance becomes increasingly important to maths, especially towards the end of Key Stage 2 with work on accurate drawing and measuring of 2-D shapes, nets of 3-D shapes and measuring for area and perimeter.

Activities

In a similar way to the previous work with different scales, gather as many different types of rulers as possible, including a metre ruler, a retractable DIY metal tape-measure, a dressmaking tape-measure, a short 10 cm or 15 cm ruler and a standard 30 cm ruler. Tell the children that rulers are a very common type of scale and they are going to use one to help them measure and draw accurately. Let the children examine the rulers, especially noticing how they are divided up. Some may still show inches and this must be explained as an old system which is not used much now. After examining the rulers, use a set with all the rulers exactly the same. Have the children find the zero position. Be careful with the zero position because many rulers have an extra piece at each end to allow for chipping. Some children will start at the very end, which will give incorrect results. Tell the children that the main marks on the rulers show units called centimetres. Write 'centimetre' on the board and explain that because mathematicians like to save time, they usually just write 'cm'. Tell them that a centimetre is about the width of a finger. Have them put their finger between the 0 and 1 divisions to check if their finger is indeed about 1 cm wide.

Give a 30 cm ruler to each child. Use the class number line to illustrate how the ruler is a small part of the whole number line. Do not say that the ruler is

the beginning of the number line as many Year 2 children will know something of negative numbers and some number lines illustrate the first negative numbers. Have the children place a finger on 0 and another finger on the 5 cm division. Tell them that this distance is 5 cm. It starts from zero and goes to five. Can they put their finger on the 3 cm mark? How about the 8 cm mark? Go through this as many times as needed as you walk around the class ensuring everyone is doing it properly.

Give the children Activity sheet 73 which shows straight lines of various lengths to the whole centimetre only. Using the school set of rulers, have the children measure each line and write the distance using the 'cm' abbreviation. Using the same sheet to record the result, allow the children to measure the length of each of their fingers to the nearest centimetre. A friend can check their results.

Ask the children to draw lines using a ruler and pencil. Tell them how long they should be. Each child puts the pencil point on the zero mark – check each child has the pencil in the correct place – then find the 4 cm division. Now tell them to move the pencil gently along from zero and stop at four. Tell them to remove the ruler and label the line with '4 cm'. Repeat this exercise with different distances.

Points to watch

Beginning measuring from the very end of the ruler. Poor pencil control.

Next step

Measure and draw lines to the nearest half centimetre.

Resources

Variety of measuring instruments including metre rules; set of 30 cm rulers

Vocabulary of time

Learning outcome

To understand and use the vocabulary of time (Y1)

Assumed knowledge and experience

This work will include the everyday vocabulary relating to time. Most very young children have an idea of concepts such as 'soon' or 'later on' but will be unsure about the length of an hour or even 5 minutes!

Mathematical importance

An understanding of the passage of time is extremely important to our everyday lives and this developing knowledge leads to accurate reading of time and working with problems that involve timings.

Activities

This is an opening awareness-raising activity. Tell the children they are going to be talking about things to do with time and you want them to tell you as many words as they can that are in some way connected with time. Tell them they must think quickly; write 'quickly' and 'quick' on the board. Ask if they can tell you what the opposite of quickly is. Write 'slow' and 'slowly'. Some prompting may be needed although they will probably come up with 'minute', 'hour', 'day', 'month' fairly readily. At some point, include 'week', 'month', 'morning', 'afternoon', 'evening', 'night', 'today', 'yesterday', 'early', 'late'. These words relate to time periods and the next step is to discuss time vocabulary that is comparative. Words should include 'faster', 'slower', 'longer', 'shorter', 'often', 'sometimes', 'usually'. Have the children make a class word bank using the words that have been offered so far.

Have the children begin to put the words discussed so far into 'real life' contexts. Discuss what they would normally do in the morning, afternoon or evening. How often they do certain things like shopping or playing a sport – use 'often', 'sometimes', 'never' and 'usually'. Write these words on the board and have each child think of one or two sentences

that go with each word. Year 1 children are unlikely to be able to write these thoughts down but some may, while some words may need to be written by an adult but they should all have a chance to say at least one sentence to the rest of the class.

One day a week or one period each day, have a 'time session'. During this session, have a device like a bell or tambourine that can be sounded if anyone says a word or phrase that relates in any way to time.

Begin to have the children estimating and comparing the length of events. These can be short term or long term. Ask the children how long the lesson is. How long has the lesson been going on? How long is left? How long do assemblies last? Are assemblies longer or shorter than lessons? How long is it until home time? If maths is now, what lesson comes later? What lesson went before art? Does PE take as long as history?

Give the children Activity sheet 74 which shows parts of the day – night, morning, afternoon, evening. Then have them write down an activity that takes place in each part of the day, for example, evening – preparing for bed.

Points to watch

Children who are finding the vocabulary of comparison difficult to use correctly.

Resources

Bell, tambourine

Next step

Ordering events. Knowing the days of the week and months of the year. Knowing the relationship between the main units of time including minutes, hours and days.

Use units of time

Learning outcome

To know the units of time and the relationship between them (Y2)

Assumed knowledge and experience

The children are likely to have a general awareness of terms such as seconds, minutes, hours and days. They may also understand the hierarchy of the units. Some work should have taken place on comparative language such as 'longer than', 'more often' and 'later'.

Mathematical importance

The children need to formalise their knowledge of the units so that they can begin to read the time and work problems with time.

Activities

By Year 2, children should know there are seven days in a week, know their names and be able to order them. Begin the activity by reminding the children of the days, then ask them how we divide up each day. The answers 'morning', 'afternoon', 'evening' and 'night' are likely to be given or should be prompted. Write these on the board in order starting from morning. Ask 'When is the morning?' and have the children begin to talk about 'between 7 and 12' or give simple definitions which use hour names. Use the class clock and the school timetable to illustrate the work. Continue through the other parts of the day. It is likely that some children's definitions will vary but arrive at a class agreement. Write this list on the board:

Morning – between 7 and 12

Afternoon – between 12 and 5

Evening – between 5 and 9

Night – between 9 and 7 the next morning

Tell the children that we use hours to divide up the day. Tell them that many lessons, including this one are about 1 hour long. Ask how many hours they think are in one day. Tell them 24 hours make one day. Using the list above to provide clues, give some times of the day and ask what they might do during those hours; for example, eleven in the morning, four in the afternoon and so on. After discussion, have each child create their own record of 'A Day in the

Life of _____'. The main group and the more able children should be able to write short sentences but the less able ones may need to use illustrations.

Moving on from hours, continue with minutes. Begin activities to establish the length of 1 minute. Use a clock with a second hand to illustrate the length of 1 minute. If a minute sand-timer is available, compare the time with that of the clock. Use stopwatches to compare a minute with clocks and sand-timers. Write on the board that an hour is made up of 60 minutes. Go through familiar events with the class and find out how long they take, for example, eating lunch (25 minutes), playtime (15 minutes), getting dressed (5 minutes). Now have the children make up individual tables.

Write '1 minute = 60 seconds' on the board. Tell the children to count to 60 by saying 'one elephant, two elephant' and have another child time them. Reverse roles. Is this a method of counting 1 minute? In the hall, ask them to jump on the spot for 1 minute while they are timed. Who jumps the most? Have the children sit in absolute silence for 1 minute. Clap your hands and after a short gap clap them again. Have the children estimate how long it is between claps. Take opportunities during the normal working day to ask general questions relating to seconds, minutes and hours; for example, how long assembly was. Did it take long to read the register? Was the music lesson about 30 minutes long?

Points to watch

Clear misunderstanding of the length of the shorter units, seconds and minutes.

Resources

Stopwatches, clocks, sand-timers

Next step

Read the time to the hour and half-hour on analogue clocks and watches.

Order events in time

Learning outcome

To order familiar events in time (Y1)

Assumed knowledge and experience

The children should have had opportunities to use basic vocabulary related to time, such as 'morning', 'soon', 'often' and 'late'. They will probably have a general awareness of other time vocabulary including units such as seconds, minutes and hours.

Mathematical importance

Sequencing events carefully will later on enable the children in solving problems relating to time.

Activities

Read the children a familiar story such as 'The Three Little Pigs'. Ask the children if they can describe the order of events using simple pictures. This may be done as a whole class. Now give the children some simple drawings of the story events which have been jumbled. The children have to order the pictures correctly. Repeat this using other well-known stories or rhymes, for example, 'Three Blind Mice', 'Goldilocks and the Three Bears'. This work may be differentiated with the more able children being given longer or more complicated stories.

Discuss with the children the order of the main events of their lives. Begin with birth and go through learning to walk, first words, toddling, pre-school and now. Illustrate simply on the board and stick to four or five main events. Use this as a basic template for the children and create a follow-up set of simply illustrated cards relating to these events. Give a set to each child along with some blank cards. Have the children fill in some important events in their own lives using illustrations, or words if possible; for example, going on a special holiday, moving house, Christmas or a birthday. Complete with the children using an activity sheet to illustrate 'My Life'.

Discuss the main events of the year. Draw or make a one calendar year timeline and display it. Have each child draw or write one thing which is significant to them during the year on the timeline. This is likely to be their birthday or a holiday but encourage them to

think of other things, for example, Bonfire Night, Easter or beginning school. Each child should cut it out and in turn come to the front to tell the class of their event and where they think it should be placed on the timeline. They can stick it there with paste. As the events are put up, discuss if they are in the correct place and how they fit with respect to those of the other children. After four or five have placed their events on the timeline, ask a few questions along the lines of 'Whose event is next to ____?', 'Are there any months with no events yet?' or 'Is ____ before or after ____?'. Over a few days, give all the children a chance to place their contribution. Do a similar exercise with the academic year.

The children will be responsible for choosing one event they want to sequence. This will need some discussion with the whole class with everyone agreeing that the task is achievable – some children are likely to select unrealistic events! They might like to think about a sporting event they know of or take part in, a home ritual, like getting dressed or ready for bed. Have some situations ready for those who need help – preparing and eating a bowl of cereal, having some toast, loading a game into a Playstation. Once selected, each child must show the sequence of the events, probably pictorially, although the main group and the most able children should be encouraged to write descriptive words or labels for the parts of the event.

Points to watch

Events out of sequence when working independently.

Resources

Timeline for one calendar year

Next step

Know in order the months of the year and the seasons.

Days of week, seasons, months

Learning outcome

To know the days of the week and the seasons (Y1)

To order the months of the year (Y2)

Assumed knowledge and experience

Most children in Years 1 and 2 will probably have heard the names of days, months and seasons but will have little idea of their relative positions or when they occur in the year. They may know a few months, such as their birth month or December.

Mathematical importance

The children are gradually learning the sequence of standard time units from seconds to year. Days of the week, seasons and names of months fit into this broadening knowledge and have many important practical applications.

Activities

Ask the children if they have ever heard the word 'season'. Do they know what it means? Do they know the names of the seasons? Ask them what season they think it is now. Begin with whichever season it is at the time and write its name on the board. Establish that seasons are most obviously related to the weather (or rather, the other way round) and that this is one of the ways we all know what season it is, as well as seeing what is happening to nature. How would the children know the seasons if they were given word clues and not pictures? Try them out with 'hot', 'cold', 'icy', 'foggy', 'dry', 'snow', 'mild', 'flowers appear', 'leaves fall', 'bare branches'. Do the same thing using pictures. Talk about how the year is divided roughly into four seasons and which months cover which seasons. This needs to be dealt with carefully as the definitions used by weather forecasters do not always match with what we can see around us!

Tell the children you know when each of them was born. Ask them to put up their hand when you say the name of the month in which they were born. Be prepared to help out a few who may not be sure! Draw a timeline divided into twelve sections but not showing the names of the months. Point out to the children that this represents one year; have them say only the names of the first and last months. Label January and December above the line and write the first names of the children born in those months below the line. Point to another section (July) without saying its name. Ask the children if they can work out which month this is. Discuss their answers, then label it July and write the appropriate children's names. Tell the children that July is about halfway through the year. Now have the children talk about special events for them which have nothing to do with birthdays; probably holidays will feature large but also Bonfire Night or Easter. Discuss the months when these happen; put them on the timeline. Talk generally about the number of days in the months and ask whether there are always the same number but there is no need for detail. Write 'February'. Continue until the timeline is complete.

Prepare a series of cards, which show the names of the months and the seasons. Give out the season cards and have the children order them. Recognise that although winter may be the obvious one to start with, the important thing is whether they are in the correct sequence. This is slightly different from the names of the months; the children should recognise that we begin with January and work through in chronological order. When the children have ordered their seasons cards, name some events with some clues about the season in which each occurs and have the children hold up the appropriate card. Do a similar exercise with the names of days and months but include questions along the lines of 'What month comes after April?', 'Which is the third month of the year?'.

Points to watch

Children who do not know the sequence after significant amounts of practice.

Resources

Pictures showing seasons

Next step

Knowing significant times of the day.

Read time to hour/half-hour (analogue)

Learning outcome

To read the time to the hour or half-hour on an analogue clock or watch (Y1)

Assumed knowledge and experience

A knowledge of some language associated with time, especially comparative words like 'before' and 'after' is expected. The children might also be used to seeing different types of clock face (analogue and digital) at home, at the shops, in school and on electrical goods.

Mathematical importance

Telling the time and writing it correctly facilitate work in other subjects, such as science and geography, and provide knowledge that can be helpful in everyday life.

Activities

Draw a circle on the board. Tell them that they have to guess what you are drawing. Put a dot in the centre. Put on marks at the 12, 3, 6 and 9 positions. Gradually add the other hour marks, then the minute-hand, hour-hand and finally the hour numbers. Tell them this is a very common sort of clock face. Ask if they know a different sort. Using the completed drawing, ask them as a group to name the parts, beginning with the whole face, then moving to the hands. Ask if they notice the difference between the two hands. Ask them how we would normally say a time; try to draw out 'o'clock'. Write '1 o'clock' on the board and tell them that 'o'' is short for 'of the'. Go around the clock with them reciting '12 o'clock', '1 o'clock', and so on. Ask them how they think we can use the hands to show the time. The children need to see that the shorter hand indicates hours while the longer one indicates minutes. If you use a geared analogue clock, turn the hands so that their movement can be seen. Point out that as the minute-hand goes around, the hour-hand covers less distance. Tell them that when the larger hand points to the 12, it is an exact hour and we call it 'o'clock'. The actual time depends upon which number the shorter hand points to. Using the geared clock, move the hands until they say 1 o'clock. Move them to ten to two, then have the children count down from 10 to 1, one at a time, until at 2 o'clock they call out together '2 o'clock'; continue around the clock.

Have three children come to the front. Give each one a ruler. Tell them that one arm is the hour-hand and the one holding the ruler is the minute-hand. Whisper that you want them to move their arms to show 3 o'clock. When they all show that time, have the rest of the class call out the time using the proper vocabulary. Repeat with 6, 9 and 12 o'clock, then have other children to the front and repeat with different times.

Using clock face stamps, have one child place the minute-hand in the upright position and the other arm as the hour-hand for six positions, then swap roles for the other six.

Talk about the times that are halfway between the whole hours. Tell them that we call these the 'half past' times. Have a child point to halfway around the clock face and make sure they all know which number the minute hand will be pointing at. Care needs to be taken. At half past, the hour-hand will have moved between two hours and children easily become confused by this. Raise the subject of clockwise and anticlockwise that may have been covered already. Point out that clock hands always go clockwise. Set the hands at 1 o'clock and move the minute-hand towards the 6. As you go, say 'this is a bit past 1', 'this is even more past 1', 'this is a lot past 1' and when you reach the 6, 'this is half past 1'. Repeat with other times. Some maths books incorrectly show the hour-hand at an exact hour position when the minute-hand is at half past.

Points to watch

Confusion between the size of the hands.

Resources

Large analogue clock face with moveable hands

Next step

Time to the quarter-hour and with digital displays.

Read quarter-hours (analogue)

Learning outcome

To read quarter-hours on an analogue clock and 12-hour digital clock and notation (Y2)

Assumed knowledge and experience

The children should have had opportunities to 'read' an analogue clock telling the hours and half-hours. They should understand the language of 'o'clock' and 'half past' as well as more general language related to time such as 'after' and 'before'. They should know that an hour is composed of 60 minutes.

Mathematical importance

This is another step in being able to read the time and show it correctly on a clock face.

Activities

Use a geared analogue clock face and remind the children of earlier work on the 'o'clock' and 'half past' times. Discuss how many minutes there are in 1 hour and talk about how many in half an hour. Ask the children how these times would be shown on a digital display. Have a digital display available if possible (the school VCR) or draw one. Discuss how the hours and half-hours are shown and particularly mention the way the hours are separated from the minutes as in, for example, 7:30. Write some times using the digital notation and have the children draw these times on to pre-stamped analogue clock faces. Reverse the process and draw some times using an analogue clock and have the children write these using digital notation – hours and half-hours only.

Begin 'quarter past' by drawing a simple analogue clock face and quartering it. Ask the children what fraction each part is. Beginning at the top, move the hands slowly until they are a quarter of the way round, then two-quarters, then three-quarters, finally back to the top. Ask the children if they can tell you how many minutes are shown at the first quarter position. Agree on 15 and tell the children that when the minute-hand points at this position – often, but not always, labelled '3' – we can either say '15 minutes past' or 'quarter past'. To begin with, ensure

that they become used to seeing the minute-hand in the particular quarter past position. Practise with on the hour, half-past and quarter-past hand positions before moving on to quarter to.

When the children are confident with the half and quarter times, move on to 'quarter past what'. Remind the children that the hands move clockwise so the quarter past hour-hand will be just leaving an hour position. Ask which hour is just being left. Practise around the clock as many times as needed. Be very careful with 'quarter to what'. The children should see that the hour-hand is closer to one hour than the other, so instead of saying which hour has been passed, as with quarter and half past, they need to become used to times that are quarter to the hour. This is a bit of a turn around for children and some become easily confused at this point. Practise the main minute-hand positions a great deal without the hour-hand. Finally, use the hour- and minute-hands together.

Relate all of the analogue quarter times to the digital display. Make one child a day responsible for spotting and saying the quarter times. The child could bang a tambourine or drum on the quarters. Give all the children a go, especially the less able ones.

Points to watch

Confusion with quarter to times.

Resources

Geared analogue clock face; digital displays

Next step

Read the time to 5 minutes on analogue and digital.

The study of shapes can be fascinating and children generally enjoy this area of study very much. Taught properly, it can be entertaining and interesting and will provide valuable insights into the world around us, along with some solid mathematical ideas.

Close observation of the simple 2-D and 3-D shapes provides a good start. Children will know these shapes from everyday life and should enjoy putting 'proper' names to them. Handling the shapes is also fun and leads easily into naming of the parts. Sorting the shapes according to attributes makes sure the children have a good grasp of names. Counting the parts, especially of 3-D shapes, provides children with lots of good practice of using good mathematical vocabulary.

Work on pattern and pictures using shape should not be underestimated as a useful mathematical tool or be relegated to a Friday afternoon.

Scrutinising pattern in shape and number is a vital skill and early work with 2-D shapes can provide excellent support to what is probably going on with number, number lines and number squares.

Symmetry appears in these early years, probably through simple folding exercises, maybe as early as the Foundation stage. Folding has natural connections with fractions and the two are often taught alongside or close to each other.

The language associated with position is vast and benefits from lots of class input backed up by general, but deliberate, use throughout the school day. Part of this work will lead into turning and from there into whole turns, half turns and quarter turns (right angles). This will develop into angle as a measure of turn and the stronger the connection is made between turn and angle, the better.

Mathematical names for 2-D/3-D shapes

Learning outcome

To describe features of familiar 2-D and 3-D objects (Y1)

To use the mathematical names for common 2-D and 3-D shapes (Y2)

Assumed knowledge and experience

The children should be used to playing with objects and in a general way will be aware of words such as 'sides' and 'edges'. They are likely to have heard of squares, rectangles and circles and be able to recognise them.

Mathematical importance

Classifying familiar shapes and beginning to define them leads on to the study of properties of more complex shapes and the use of instruments to draw them.

Activities

Give out coloured plastic shapes to each table. Let the children have a minute to play with them without any guidance. Ask the children to choose one shape and draw around it. Now the children should put the shape to one side and be prepared to give you one word that describes something about their shape. In turn, have four or five children stand up, hold up the shape and describe it. Choose children with different shapes. As the descriptions go on, quickly draw each shape on the board and enter the words that have been offered alongside the shapes. When this has been completed, take each shape one at a time, refer to the board and ask the rest of the class for more words that describe the shape. Gradually build up word lists for each shape. Begin to draw up a word bank connected with descriptions of 2-D shapes. Words such as 'flat', 'straight', 'curved', 'sides', 'bent', 'corners', 'edges' are likely to have been offered and some may not be appropriate. Place the word bank somewhere on the wall where it is obvious and can be referred to.

With the 2-D shapes, have each table choose one of each shape and put the rest away in a tray. Give the children a minute to name the shapes among themselves. If they do not know the proper name they must invent one! The children from one group should choose a shape, hold it up and say its name.

If it's an amusing made-up name, so much the better. Discuss the name if it is correct, draw the shape on the board and label it. Repeat around the tables until the main shapes have been chosen: circle, square, rectangle and triangle. The tray may also include semicircles. Year 2 children may be using hexagons, pentagons and octagons. Draw the shapes and give them a title and place them near the word bank.

If your maths groups are differentiated, give the groups the names of the shapes. The less able children may have the circles, the main group the triangles and the more able children the rectangles.

The children on one table should choose a 2-D shape from the pile and conceal it under a book. The activity involves giving a group of children on another table clues about the shape until they guess the shape; for example, it has straight sides, it has four sides, two sides are the same length. Repeat this so that each table has a turn.

Discuss and work with 3-D shapes in a similar way, building a word bank and display. Use a bag that the children cannot see through. Secretly place a 3-D shape into the bag and bring a child to the front. Have the child describe the shape by touch only to the rest of the class. Repeat with different shapes. Insist on the correct language.

Points to watch

Poor use of mathematical language.

Resources

Coloured plastic 2-D shapes; 3-D shapes

Next step

A wider range of 2-D and 3-D shapes.

Make models, patterns and pictures

Learning outcome

To make and describe models, patterns and pictures (Y1)

Assumed knowledge and experience

The children are likely to have had opportunities to make pictures and models with sticky shapes or construction kits. This work encourages them to repeat these activities but with a deliberate emphasis on using the appropriate mathematical vocabulary.

Mathematical importance

Recognising pattern and shape within patterns and models leads to a deepening understanding of the properties of shapes.

Activities

A number of easily available computer programs include work where the children can drag and drop shapes and make patterns. Some programs use teddy bears and non-geometric shapes which are probably more suitable for earlier work at the Foundation stage but others provide excellent work in creating patterns and pictures.

Use one of each of the main shapes and place them so that their edges touch. Draw around the whole shape and produce an outline that can be shown on the OHP. Give out the 2-D shapes and have the children use them to attempt to duplicate the outline. This work can be differentiated fairly easily and the more able children may be given outline shapes of some complexity to deal with.

Give the children an activity sheet of a prepared pattern for them to complete by continuation.

Draw on the board simple pictures using 2-D shapes, for example, a stylised face, house, tree, boat, train. Working in pairs, the children must use the plastic shapes to reproduce your drawing. One child will make the copy and has to ask for the shape they need using the correct names. The other child must select the correct shape and pass it to the first child.

Give out construction bricks to each table and have the children join them together in a pattern that is shown on the board. These patterns might start with an alternating red/yellow/red/yellow sequence; move on to red/red/yellow/yellow, then more complicated examples, such as red/yellow/yellow/red/yellow/yellow. This work is easily differentiated. After some examples you give them, have the children develop their own patterns. The children's own patterns should be described to an adult or the rest of the class at some point. Allow children to present their patterns to friends for continuation.

Have each child select a solid shape from a square-based pyramid, triangular-based pyramid, cube or cuboid. They should now try to reproduce this shape using construction materials such as flexible-jointed kits, straws or pipe-cleaners. Ask the children why it would be difficult to make a sphere using these materials. Is there any way they could create a sphere? You may want to have them blowing bubbles!

Have photos available of 3-D shapes, some simple, some taken from unusual angles. The children must identify the 3-D counterparts and name them.

Points to watch

Failure to recognise the correct drawing to fill in a gap in a pattern.

Resources

OHP; 2-D plastic shapes; 3-D solid shapes

Next step

Using a wider variety of shapes and combining them, especially cubes.

Sort shapes and describe features

Learning outcome

To sort shapes and describe some of their features (Y2)

Assumed knowledge and experience

The children should have worked with the main 2-D shapes and some of the 3-D solids. They should know their names and some of their properties. In general terms, the children should understand about sorting into groups based upon given criteria.

Mathematical importance

Being able to sort and classify shapes shows a good understanding of definitions and correct use of vocabulary.

Activities

Give out the plastic 2-D shapes and after giving the children a minute to play with the shapes, ask them to name the shapes and the parts. They should be used to naming the sides and corners. The children should also be able to tell you if the surface is flat or rough (some plastic shapes have a dimpled surface). Some children will call a surface of a 2-D shape, a side, so they will say a rectangle has two sides – a top and a bottom. This is incorrect and needs to be addressed. On 2-D shapes, the correct name for a place where two lines meet is a vertex (plural, vertices). However, some teachers call the point where two lines meet on a 2-D shape a corner and where edges meet on a 3-D shape, vertices. Go through all of the common 2-D shapes naming the parts. Have each child draw around each 2-D shape and label the sides, face and corners.

Each group should have a selection of 2-D shapes in front of them. Tell the children that you want them to sort out the shapes in some way. The way is up to them but they must be able to explain to everyone else how they have done it and they only have 2 minutes to work it out. After 2 minutes, go around each group. The children must explain how they have grouped the shapes. Make a note of their methods on the board. Some may be a bit strange; children often come up with peculiar methods! The proper sorting methods should be written on the board. These

should include, sorting by straight or curved sides, sorting by the number of sides, sorting by the number of corners and possibly sorting by symmetry. Have the children mix up the shapes and sort them in a different way. The main group and more able children should be able to create their own table and write the names of the shapes in the appropriate headings with a title that suggests the sorting criteria they have used. The less able ones may be given a table with the criteria already on but instead of writing in the names they may draw around the shapes.

Give the children some homework (if the school homework policy allows!) of collecting over a couple of weeks, containers or objects that are spheres, cubes, cuboids, cylinders, pyramids, or cones. Try to build up a collection and have some others available in the classroom. Make a display of these objects.

Using some 3-D solid shapes, ask the children to first name the shape and then name the parts. Distribute the collection of containers and objects and have the children match them with the school set. Make sure each child has at least one shape. Each child should hold up their shape and then you ask them to count the number of faces. Say 'Hold up your shape if it has six faces', or 'Hold up your shape if it has less than five faces', and so on.

Points to watch

Counting edges and vertices on 3-D shapes can be confusing!

Resources

2-D and 3-D shapes; 3-D containers and objects that represent cubes

Next step

Sorting 3-D shapes by vertices and edges.

Folding shapes and beginning symmetry

Learning outcome

To fold shapes in half and begin symmetry (Y1)

Assumed knowledge and experience

The children will have worked with some 2-D shapes and will probably know the names of the more common ones such as rectangle, square, circle and triangle. They should be familiar working with paper and cutting out. Some work on halves and halving may have been carried out.

Mathematical importance

The various sorts of symmetry provide interesting insights into shape and their uses (both 2-D and 3-D) as well as providing another categorisation for enabling sorting to take place.

Activities

Put some rectangular pieces of cut-up sugar paper on each table. The exact size does not matter but somewhere between A5 and A4 would be suitable. Tell the children you are going to fold a piece of paper in half. The vocabulary of half and halving should have been taught by this point but if it has not, this work may be used as an introduction. Take a large piece of sugar paper (A3) and tell the children you are going to fold it in half. Fold the sheet in a way that is clearly not in half, with a very small section and a very large one. Show it to the children and ask them if you have folded the paper in half. Agree that it is not in half and begin to draw out definitions of half. Once a definition has been agreed, begin to explore with the children how the paper might be halved. Bring out the point that each half must be exactly the same size. Model this for the children and show them how to make a sharp crease on the fold line. Let each child have a piece of the paper and try folding it in half. Have the children check each other's work. When this has been done, draw a rectangle on the board and label each half with '½' and 'half'; also label the fold as 'fold line'. The children may complete this activity by labelling their own paper.

Repeat the activity with paper cut into squares, circles, and equilateral and isosceles triangles. The circle can prove difficult both mentally and physically for some

children in finding the fold line. The children should label the paper as before. Every child should end up with at least one of each shape. This work, if done using coloured paper, can make a very attractive display.

Most of the children should be able to find more than one fold line on each shape. Have the children try to find different fold lines to those already used. Most children will easily fold vertical and horizontal lines for the rectangle and may then try the diagonals. Children often need to be pointed towards the diagonals for the square. The equilateral triangle can be difficult. Pay attention to how they get on with the circle that has an infinite number of fold lines.

Give the children some simple line drawings of rectangles, squares, triangles and circles (see Activity sheet 83). According to the National Numeracy Strategy, the idea of a line of symmetry is not introduced until Year 2 but most Year 1 and some Foundation stage children easily pick up the idea. Have the children examine each shape and supposed fold line on the activity sheet and put a tick if they think it is correct and a cross if not. Some may be able to draw on the correct fold lines.

Points to watch

Poor folding skills leading to confusion about halving.

Resources

A3 paper; A4 and A5 (approximate) sugar or coloured paper

Next step

Lines of symmetry. Introduction of the idea of mirror lines and reflective symmetry.

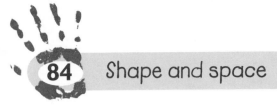

Line symmetry

Learning outcome

To begin to recognise line symmetry (Y2)

Assumed knowledge and experience

The children should have worked with folding paper in halves. They should know the meaning of half and halving and be able to recognise fold lines on the common 2-D shapes. The children should also know the names of the common 2-D shapes.

Mathematical importance

This work has children examining the detail of symmetry, leading to mirror lines and reflection with more complicated shapes.

Activities

Remind the children of folding paper into halves. Make sure they know that the two halves have to be equal and that the line that creates the halves is called the fold line. It may be appropriate to revise the fact that most of the simple shapes looked at so far have more than one fold line.

A number of computer programs allow children to draw or paint a pattern on the screen and then reflect it in one or more mirror lines (Colour Magic). Although this activity is rather simple because the computer does all the work, it does give a very good idea of reflection on a line. The printouts make a good display.

Ask the children to bring into school a small object or toy. A selection of such items needs to be available for those who do not bring anything. Give a mirror to each child. Some commercially available mirrors are rather small; A5 is most suitable. Show the children how to hold the mirror vertically to the desk top and let them experiment with their object and the mirror by moving the mirror towards and away from the object and moving either the object or the mirror to a different relevant angle. Now use a fairly large object and a suitably sized mirror (one brought in from home may be best) and show the children how you can move the mirror in front of the object to make interesting views. When the mirror is aligned to one

edge of the object, the object appears double. Move the mirror slightly over the object. The children should notice the image is slightly smaller than the object. Ask the children if they think they could move the mirror so that it appeared as though there was only one of the object. Have a few children come to the front and experiment. Try the same with a few of their faces – always keeping safety issues in mind.

Have the children work in pairs. Give each group a piece of string about 30 cm long and put a selection of plastic shapes on each table. The children must place the string on the table, at right angles to them. Tell them that the string represents a mirror line. One child takes a plastic shape and puts it adjacent to the string. Their partner must then replicate the image on the other side of the line. The children take it in turns, gradually building up a more complex picture. If a camera or digital camera is available, take a few photos for evidence and display purposes. The more able children could use some of the coloured plastic shapes that are often used for work with tessellation. Make a collection of pictures of objects, animals and signs. Photocopy this and give out copies. Have the children draw lines of symmetry. Faces and animals are rarely, if ever, exactly symmetrical. This needs to be pointed out.

Points to watch

Misplacement of the mirror line.

Resources

Mirrors – plastic are suitable; coloured plastic shapes; tessellating coloured plastic shapes; large mirror; string

Next step

Completing drawings when half the picture is given with a mirror line.

Describe position, direction, movement

Learning outcome

To use everyday language to describe position, direction and movement (Y1)

Assumed knowledge and experience

The children are likely to have heard such expressions as 'over there', 'come here', 'where is ____?', and so on. They should have a good understanding of other everyday vocabulary including 'after', 'next to' and 'close'.

Mathematical importance

An accurate description of position is an important life skill and leads to work with coordinates, reflection, rotation and transposition.

Activities

This activity can be ongoing through the year. Start the children off by having them line up on the playground. Stand at the front of the line facing them and tell them that you are in front of them. Now turn away from them and tell them that they are behind you. Go up and down the line asking individuals or groups who is in front of or behind them. This activity can be done in PE or games when the children are queuing to use apparatus.

When the children are in a line facing forward, have them turn either to the left or right. Join in the line and face the same direction as the children. Tell them 'George is standing beside me on my left' (or right, as the case may be). Move to a different position in the line and repeat the exercise. Move out of the line and have the children tell you who is on their left or right. This activity could also be carried out in circle time. Repeat the activity but ask the children if they can think of another way of saying 'beside'. Prompt towards 'next to', then intermix 'next to' and 'beside'.

Have the children sit in two rows facing each other. Sit down in one row and revise 'next to' and 'beside'. Introduce the idea of 'opposite'. Name the child that you are opposite. Make it clear that you are opposite each other. Ask opposite pairs to stand up. Ask children to say who is beside/next to them on left/right and opposite.

The children should stand in two rows opposite each other. Join on the end of one row. Say that you are going to walk towards the other line, then do it. When you are close to the line, stop and say you are going to walk away from the line. Return to the starting position. Have the whole line walk towards the opposite line, then walk away from it. Let the other line have a go. Have individuals or groups walk towards and away from their friends.

The children should sit in a circle. Sit with them. Tell them that you are going to walk around the circle. Stand up, walk around it and return to your place. Have a few other children do the same. Now tell them that you are going to walk around the circle but cut through it and return to your place. Do this emphasising 'through' as you do it. Have the children do the same thing and say when they go through. This is similar to the well-known children's game sometimes called Duck, Duck, Goose.

Use a number line. Point to the numbers 2 and 3 and say that these are close to each other. Have the children suggest other combinations that are close. Now point to the 2 and the 99 and say that they are far apart. Ask the children to make other combinations that are far apart. The 1–100 number squares and number lines may be used for: position, above, below, before, after, middle, centre, edge, corner, top, bottom, side, direction, up, down, forwards, backwards, sideways, across, to and from.

Points to watch

Any confusion of terms after lots of opportunities to hear them and put into practice.

Resources

PE hall; 1–100 number square; 1–100 number line

Next step

Clockwise and anticlockwise.

Turning clockwise/anticlockwise

Learning outcome

To talk about things that turn, make whole turns and half turns (Y1 and Y2)

To recognise whole, half and quarter turns to the left/right, clockwise/anticlockwise (Y1 and Y2)

To know that a right angle is a measure of quarter turn (Y1 and Y2)

Assumed knowledge and experience

The children should have worked with some vocabulary concerning position and movement. They are likely to have heard of turn and turning through everyday life and within the classroom, for example, 'turn and face me please'.

Mathematical importance

Turning and the amount of turn leads to work on angles.

Activities

Stand in the centre of the classroom with arms together pointing forward at a child. Tell the children that you are facing (name of child) but you are going to turn and face another child. Repeat this a few times. Ask the children if you are making a big turn or a small turn. Make a very small turn and ask the children again. Now make a large turn (about 180°) and ask again. Now select a child to come to the centre and take your place. Begin by having the child say how they are going to turn, that is, a big or small turn. Repeat this with a few more children. Now have another child as a demonstrator but this time the rest of the children can give instructions such as 'Make a large/small turn' or 'Turn to point at ____'.

Begin to talk about amounts of turns. Have the children sit in a circle and stand at the centre. Use a metre stick or pointer and point towards one child. Tell the children you are going to make one whole turn and ask them who they think you will be pointing at. Repeat starting with different children. Do not mention clockwise and anticlockwise at this point. Repeat similar activities with half turns and quarter turns.

When half turns have been fully discussed and quarter turns are underway, tell the children that we have a special name for these. Tell them we call quarter turns right angles. Demonstrate by turning yourself and showing what a quarter turn, a right angle, looks like.

If the classroom has a door, open the door so that it makes a right angle with the opening. The children must realise that a right angle is the measure of the amount of turn. Draw a right angle on the board and show the children some examples of right angles from around the room, for example, corners of the room, corners of books or tables. Have the children draw some right angles using a ruler and give some other examples they can find in the room. Use plastic shapes and have the children recognise right angles.

Using construction kits and other resources, make a display of things that turn. Point out to the children that some things turn around a point, for example, hands of a clock, whereas others may turn around a line, for example, a door or pages of a book. This work could link with the QCA exemplar topic entitled Winding up.

Use a geared display clock if available. Move the hands of the clock in the normal direction and tell the children that we call this direction of movement 'clockwise' because it is the way the hands of the clock move. Have a few children move the hands around clockwise. Now move the hands in the reverse direction and ask the children what they think this might be called. They are likely to say 'backwards'. Tell the children that we call this direction 'anticlockwise'.

Points to watch

Mixing clockwise and anticlockwise.

Resources

Construction kits; geared display clock; plastic 2-D shapes

Next step

The compass points. Beginning to work with coordinates.

Right angles

Learning outcome

To recognise right angles in rectangles and squares (Y2)

Assumed knowledge and experience

The children should have discussed quarter turns prior to this work when dealing with the topic of turning. They may have been told that a quarter turn can be called a right angle and have seen examples in the environment around them and at home.

Mathematical importance

This leads on to more general work on angles – measuring, drawing – and knowing about angles in triangles and quadrilaterals.

Activities

Remind the children about turns, especially the quarter turn. Tell them that the special name for a quarter turn is a right angle. Point out a few right angles in the room, for example, door corners, book covers, and give the children a few minutes to spot as many as they can. Their observations may be recorded in writing or by drawing. Individual whiteboards would be useful if available. Collect the children's ideas and produce a 'Right Angle Collection' of words, objects and descriptions, either on a large piece of paper or as part of a display.

Share out the 2-D plastic geometric shapes between the tables. Make sure a large selection is available, including triangles and circles. The main group and more able children might also have a selection of the 2-D tessellating shapes that will increase the variety. Begin by having the children play with the shapes for a minute. After this, tell them they are to sort the shapes according to the following criteria: shapes with right angles and shapes without right angles. Draw a line down the centre of several large pieces of sugar paper and label the columns appropriately on each sheet for this prior to the lesson and give them out to groups of children. Give the children 5 minutes to sort their shapes and put them on the paper in the correct columns, then have them quickly draw around the shapes and put them to one side. Ask a group to

bring their sheet to the front and discuss their results. When the first group have finished, ask the others if they need to change any of their shapes to the other column. Have another group come to the front and discuss their results.

Put out joining strips and connectors on each table. Have each child connect two strips of the same size at the ends. The strips should be placed over each other so that they appear as one. Tell the children to imagine these are the hands of a clock. Let them move the 'hands' one complete turn, then half a turn. Finally, tell them to put the strips into a right angle shape by making a quarter turn. Check that each child has produced a right angle. Now have the children go around the classroom using their own right angles to check out others they see. If possible, each child or group of children can make a list of their discoveries.

Prepare an activity sheet that contains a selection of geometric and random shapes (see Activity sheet 87). Draw a random shape on the board that has just one right angle. Ask the children to spot the right angle. When it has been identified, place a small neat cross inside the angle. Tell the children they have to do the same thing on each shape on their activity sheets.

Points to watch

Inaccurate making of right angles with the joining strips.

Resources

Individual whiteboards; 2-D plastic shapes

Next step

Knowing that a straight line is two right angles. Recognising angles that are greater than or less than a right angle.

Use of number lines and number sticks

Children should be introduced to the idea of a number line as early as possible. To begin with, the line may go from 1 to 10 or even less (5) for some children. Zero may appear and, depending on the class, will not cause much consternation. Children are used to the idea of 'none' and can generally equate the idea of one less than 1 being zero.

The number line may be extended as the children's mathematical knowledge develops but the usual next step is 20. Some teachers find it helpful to have an intermediary step of 14. After 20, 31 is a useful extension because it crosses the 30 boundary, often relates to the total number of children (and staff) in the room and can be associated with the number of days in some of the months.

The structure of the line beyond 20 is up to the individual teacher and their knowledge of the class but most teachers will move to 100 and have the number square as well. Counting on in multiples of 5 and 10 requires a line to 100.

Introducing negative numbers often takes place in the infants. Children find this concept less difficult than adults often imagine. Going down to a small number like –4 will provide a good start and is enough to teach the concept.

Number sticks can be used in a variety of ways. In early mathematical work, they may be used as a 3-D display of the number line, enabling you to hold it, move it around, point to positions and have the children work with it. The sections can represent any multiple you choose, so it can be used with early work on counting in steps and multiples.

The number stick is particularly useful when working with multiplication tables. The first and second sections represent 1× and 2× with the tenth representing 10×. The visual nature of the stick means that children can easily see the halfway mark (5×) and from there work out the 4× and 6×. After a while, pointing at positions should enable a quick response.

Number line from 1 to 20

Number line from 1 to 31

Number line from 1 to 100

Number line from –4 to 100

Simple number stick

Use of number squares

The 1–100 square (see *Blueprints Maths Key Stage 1: Pupil Resource Book* page 88 which is photocopiable) is a marvellous resource for helping to teach number. Once children begin to know numbers up to 10, the square can be introduced as another visual aid to support learning. Children find the shape itself interesting and will often look at the numbers just for the fun of spotting simple patterns. To begin with, these patterns are likely to be very basic and include spotting the multiples of 5 and tens. Later on, work with counting in steps, multiples and observing connections and visually highlighting them using markers will assist patterns.

Blank 1–100 number squares are extremely useful and can be used in many ways. One number may be placed on the square, for example, 31, and the children asked to count on or back in regular steps backwards and forwards from it or to write the numbers which surround 31. A square may be pointed out and the children asked to say the appropriate number. Numbers in a specific multiplication table can be

written on and the children invited to examine the patterns. Small magnetic number squares, 1–100 and blanks, are available for use with individual whiteboards.

Number squares may be used for showing addition and subtraction visually, especially when interesting stickers or magnets are used to highlight the numbers in question. The blank square may be used in smaller sections with the teacher drawing a matrix and producing small problems such as shown here:

+	5	7	12
4			
7			

The variations are endless and three differentiated matrices may be drawn on the same board.

1	2	3	4	5	6	7	8	9	10
11	12	13	14	15	16	17	18	19	20
21	22	23	24	25	26	27	28	29	30
31	32	33	34	35	36	37	38	39	40
41	42	43	44	45	46	47	48	49	50
51	52	53	54	55	56	57	58	59	60
61	62	63	64	65	66	67	68	69	70
71	72	73	74	75	76	77	78	79	80
81	82	83	84	85	86	87	88	89	90
91	92	93	94	95	96	97	98	99	100

Use of number fans/coin fans

Number fans are a way of eliciting easily visible, quick responses from children. In reply to a question, each child produces the answer on the fan and the whole class show their answers to you. You quickly look around the room to see any mistakes. At its simplest, the fans can be used to answer simple questions such as 'What number is one more than ____?'. The children position the numbers on the fan to show the answer. To begin with, young children might find the handling of the fan difficult and this can take some of the pace out of a lesson. However, with some practice, children do become used to moving the fan more quickly and the advantage of the quick response becomes apparent. Number fans can contain different sets of numbers and older children may need a set containing a decimal point.

Coin fans are commercially available and may be used with younger children when working with money. Coin fans need a decimal point so that decimal notation can be taught during the infant stage.

Coin fans can be made within school; templates are available in *Blueprints Maths Key Stage* 1: *Pupil Resource Book* pages 89 and 90. They can be very time consuming to make and some care has to be given to the type of fixing used. Nexus makes very good quality number and coin fans and, although fairly expensive, they will last a long time.

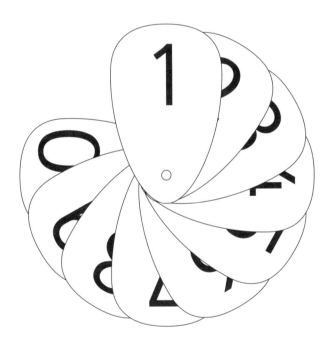

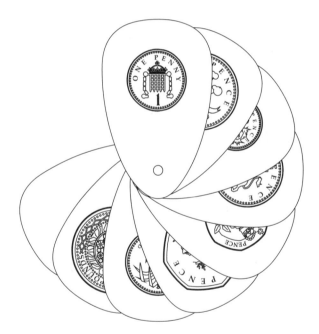

Use of individual whiteboards

Much like the slates and chalk of old, children can use individual whiteboards so that they can do working out and give responses to questions in a simple form. The boards are commercially available in A4 and A5 sizes and it is an advantage if they have a surface which can take magnetic materials such as number squares and numbers.

The boards can be used in a number of ways.

Firstly, they can be very useful when the teacher or LSA is working with a small group. The children can perform the task on the board and, because the writing will be fairly large, the teacher can easily see around the group and check the procedure is being carried out properly. Once the procedure has been checked, the board can be wiped clean for the next part of the lesson. If a stage of the work is especially important, the work can be copied into the maths book for reference.

Secondly, the boards can be used for the children to write their answers on, especially at the start of lessons where mental arithmetic is often carried out. With the answers written, the children simply hold up the boards to face you. Now,

rather than going around looking at books or only hearing a few spoken answers, the whole class can be checked in seconds. The boards can then be wiped for the next question. As with number fans, the pace of a lesson can slacken when the boards are first used but most children soon pick up speed and the motivation of using something different compensates for the slight falling away of speed which may happen at the start.

Working with the boards also has the advantage of cutting down on marking although this should not be seen as a strong educational reason for purchasing them!

Laminated sheets from DIY centres can be cut up to make the boards. This produces a cheap product but the surfaces can be easily damaged, especially when piled up at the end of lessons. Different types of markers also need to be experimented with on the self-made boards. Good-quality boards are more expensive but Nexus makes a particularly good one. The board has a solid surround which stops the board surface being rubbed when stacked. Markers and erasers are also available.

Record sheet (class teacher)

Child's name	Number names to 20	Number names to 31	Number names to 100	Counting to 20/31	Counting to 100	Counting in ones/tens and hundreds	Counting from any two-digit number	Counting in twos	Odds and evens	Steps of five and three	Steps of three, four and five	Multiples of 2, 5 and 10	Read and write numbers 20/100	Partitioning	0 as place holder

Record sheet (class teacher)

Child's name	Reinforcing activities	Comparing and ordering	Ordinal numbers	More than, less than, between	The = sign and comparing	One more or less	Ten or hundred more or less	Order whole numbers to 100	Sensible guesses to 20/50, vocabulary	Rounding to nearest ten	Half and quarter	Equivalence	Understanding addition	Addition in any order	Using the + sign

Record sheet (class teacher)

Child's name	Number sentences	Symbols for unknown numbers	Adding two or more numbers	Adding three two-digit numbers	Understanding subtraction	Vocabulary of subtraction	The – sign; symbols for unknown numbers	Recording calculations using symbols	Using symbols in number sentences	Addition/subtraction as inverse operations	Addition in different order	Checking	Number pairs totalling ten/bond bingo	Multiples of 10 totalling 100	Addition doubles and halves to 10

Record sheet (class teacher)

Child's name	Subtraction facts to 10	Number bonds to 10 (+ and −)	2x and 10x tables	Multiplication facts for 5× table	Division, 2x, 10x tables/10-multiples halves	Doubles to 15/doubles of multiples of 5	Multiplication as repeated addition	Division as grouping	Multiply and divide with confidence	Choosing operations, efficient methods	Solve simple puzzles and problems	Explain how problems are solved	Patterns and relationships	Explain in writing and orally	Solving 'real life' problems

Record sheet (class teacher)

Child's name	Recognise coins of different values	Find total, give change	Choose which coins	Paying exact sums using small coins	Translate between pounds and pennies	Sort objects – lists and tables	Sort and classify – pictures/pictograms	Sort and classify – lists	Simple block graphs	Estimate, measure, compare size	Estimate, measure, compare size/capacity	Read simple scales to nearest division	Measure/draw to the nearest centimetre	Vocabulary of time	Use units of time

Record sheet (class teacher)

Child's name	Order events in time	Days of week, seasons, months	Read time to hour/half-hour (analogue)	Read quarter-hours (analogue)	Mathematical names for 2-D/3-D shapes	Make models, patterns and pictures	Sort shapes and describe features	Folding shapes and beginning symmetry	Line symmetry	Describe position, direction, movement	Turning clockwise/anticlockwise	Right angles			

Record sheet (supply teacher)

	School										
Number names to 20											
Number names to 31											
Number names to 100											
Counting to 20/31											
Counting to 100											
Counting in ones/tens and hundreds											
Counting from any two-digit number											
Counting in twos											
Odds and evens											
Steps of five and three											
Steps of three, four and five											
Multiples of 2, 5 and 10											
Read and write numbers 20/100											
Partitioning											
0 as place holder											
Reinforcing activities											
Comparing and ordering											
Ordinal numbers											
More than, less than, between											
The = sign and comparing											
One more or less											
Ten or hundred more or less											

Record sheet (supply teacher)

	School									
Order whole numbers to 100										
Sensible guesses to 20/50, vocabulary										
Rounding to nearest ten										
Half and quarter										
Equivalence										
Understanding addition										
Addition in any order										
Using the + sign										
Number sentences										
Symbols for unknown numbers										
Adding two or more numbers										
Adding three two-digit numbers										
Understanding subtraction										
Vocabulary of subtraction										
The – sign; symbols for unknown numbers										
Recording calculations using symbols										
Using symbols in number sentences										
Addition/subtraction as inverse operations										
Addition in different order										
Checking										
Number pairs totalling ten/bond bingo										
Multiples of 10 totalling 100										

Record sheet (supply teacher)

	School								
Addition doubles and halves to 10									
Subtraction facts to 10									
Number bonds to 10 (+ and −)									
2× and 10× tables									
Multiplication facts for 5× table									
Division, 2×, 10× tables/10-multiples halves									
Doubles to 15/doubles of multiples of 5									
Multiplication as repeated addition									
Division as grouping									
Multiply and divide with confidence									
Choosing operations, efficient methods									
Solve simple puzzles and problems									
Explain how problems are solved									
Patterns and relationships									
Explain in writing and orally									
Solving 'real life' problems									
Recognise coins of different values									
Find total, give change									
Choose which coins									
Paying exact sums using small coins									
Translate between pounds and pennies									
Sort objects – lists and tables									

Record sheet (supply teacher)

	School									
Sort and classify – pictures/pictograms										
Sort and classify – lists										
Simple block graphs										
Estimate, measure, compare size										
Estimate, measure, compare size/capacity										
Read simple scales to nearest division										
Measure/draw to the nearest centimetre										
Vocabulary of time										
Use units of time										
Order events in time										
Days of week, seasons, months										
Read time to hour/half-hour (analogue)										
Read quarter-hours (analogue)										
Mathematical names for 2-D/3-D shapes										
Make models, patterns and pictures										
Sort shapes and describe features										
Folding shapes and beginning symmetry										
Line symmetry										
Describe position, direction, movement										
Turning clockwise/anticlockwise										
Right angles										